HUGH CARPENTER & TERI SANDISON

TEN SPEED PRESS

TEN SPEED PRESS
Post Office Box 7123
Berkeley, California 94707

Cover and book design by Beverly Wilson
Typography by Scott Woodworth
Typefaces used in this book are Avant Garde, Futura and Vanilla.

Library of Congress Cataloging-in-Publication Data
Carpenter, Hugh
Hot Wok/Hugh Carpenter and Teri Sandison; photography by Teri Sandison.
    p. cm.
Includes index.
ISBN 0-89815-678-5 (pbk.)
1. Wok cookery. 2. Stir frying. 3. Cookery, Oriental.
I. Sandison, Teri. II. Title.
TX840. W65C37 1995
641.7'7–dc20   94-45004
                            CIP

First printing 1995
Printed in China
    3 4 5 - 99 98 97 96 95

To teachers and students...

A GOOD TEACHER IS BUT THE MIRROR: THE TEACHER REFLECTS THE STUDENTS' LIGHT TO LIGHT THEIR PATH.

Contents

Hot Wok Night After Night

Here is the hot wok story and the amazingly easy steps for becoming a stir-fry master. No other pan works as well as a wok for stir-frying and no other cooking technique better meets our fast-paced, health-conscious society's need for quick-to-prepare, flavor-intense food.

Today's wok, no different than the millions of Chinese woks that have been used to create one of the world's great cuisines, yields gastronomic triumphs, whether in the form of a simple vegetable stir-fry on a workday night or as seared lamb rolled inside Chinese flour wrappers for a weekend gathering. Wisps of smoke drift from the metal surface, scallops sizzle dramatically, vegetables capsize in rapid action, and the kitchen aromas announce the arrival of each Hot Wok dish.

The hot wok stir-fry is a dance, a blur of motion, as the stir-fry cook at work becomes enveloped in a world of sight, sound, smell, and taste. There are no long moments for thoughtful tastings and the adjustment of seasonings, no opportunities to re-read cooking instructions or complete preparation steps as food sears in the wok. Hot woks demand action and cooking by instinct, which means moving rhythmically, listening to the cooking sounds, watching the food change color, shaking the wok with both hands to loosen the food so it slips from the wok with ease, splashing rice wine to moisten a vegetable, and stir-tossing the wok's contents again and again in a few brief minutes.

Flavor-intense food is the crowning achievement of wok cooking. The high heat caramelizes the sugars in vegetables, sears and browns meat while evaporating the marinades into flavorful-intense essences, and flash-cooks seafood so the ocean flavor is locked inside before the exterior has a chance to toughen. Adding to the flavor complexity, the high notes of aromatic seasonings, such as minced fresh ginger, garlic, orange zest, and serrano chiles, as well as the last-minute splash of stir-fry sauces, cause a dish's flavor profile to change with each bite.

It is these flavorful rewards that prompt us to turn to stir-fry dishes night after night. If you are starting out with stir-frying, read the next section, Hot Wok Equipment, and then begin cooking the recipes. As you become more familiar with stir-fry techniques, read the book's other brief explanatory sections to further your understanding and, possibly, to prepare you to improvise your own wok dishes. Along the way, we provide practical menu suggestions, give lots of presentation ideas, and offer a troubleshooting section for solving stir-fry problems that occur. We think you'll agree that wok cooking is not only easy and inexpensive, but a creative, healthful and flavorful way to cook for family and friends.

Hugh Carpenter and Teri Sandison

oks are practical, simple cooking vessels that have been used for thousands of years in China to create a vast range of superb recipes. With their sloping, concave sides, woks require less oil for cooking than frying pans and, when given a stir, ingredients automatically fall to the lower, hottest part of the wok for quick, even cooking difficult to duplicate in other pans. However, there is a huge range of quality in woks. If you lack the type of wok recommended below, use a heavy 14-inch cast-iron skillet.

Hot Wok Equipment

Hot Woks

Buy the heaviest, 14- or 16-inch flat-bottom wok you can find, with one long handle and a second shorter handle on the opposite edge. Woks that work well range from the inexpensive, traditional heavy steel type sold in Asian markets, to the modern stainless-steel, nonstick, and copper woks available at gourmet cookware shops. Avoid electric woks because they never generate the high heat necessary to properly sear ingredients. In addition, avoid woks that only have two short handles (because the hand that stabilizes the wok during stir-frying will undoubtedly get burnt), or woks that have just one handle (their weight and awkward shape make it impossible to easily slide the food out of the wok). Lastly, never buy miniature woks. These tiny woks, measuring 8 to 12 inches in diameter, do not have enough surface area to maintain proper heat—even when cooking small quantities.

Whether stir-frying on a gas or electric stove, always use a flat-bottom wok because a larger surface area will come into contact with the heat than if you use a traditionally shaped round-bottom wok. Flat-bottom woks work equally well on gas and electric stoves, but round-bottom woks only work well on gas stoves. When placed on an electric burner, so little of the rounded bottom comes into contact with the electric coil, that the wok quickly loses essential heat during the stir-fry process. When using the round-bottom wok on gas stoves, place the wok directly on the gas grate, or, if the flames will not be extinguished, invert the grate or remove it and rest the round-bottom wok directly on the burner so the flames leap up around the sides of the wok. Never elevate the wok on a "wok ring," which produces boiled rather than stir-fried food.

Heavy steel woks require special care and an initial seasoning. To season a new wok, scrub it thoroughly inside and out with hot soapy water. Dry the wok, then place it over high heat. When the wok becomes hot to the touch, add ¼ cup cooking oil (peanut or canola oil) to the center. With a paper towel and spoon, coat the inside surface with oil; just as the oil begins to smoke slightly, remove the wok from the heat. Let it cool completely, then wipe all the oil from the wok. With repeated use, the seasoned wok will gradually acquire a beautiful black nonstick luster. It is this black "seasoning" that contributes a special flavor to *Hot Wok* dishes. Provided no one scrubs off the seasoning, and the wok is only used for stir-frying, it will never need to be seasoned again.

To clean a heavy steel wok, place it in a sink and fill with hot water. After it has soaked a few minutes, or after the meal is finished, use hot water, a little dish soap, and a soft sponge to rub off all food particles that remain stuck to the sides. Never scrub the wok with an abrasive pad, because this will quickly strip off the seasoning. Dry the wok over medium heat, then store. Do not oil the inside surface before storing, because this oil will eventually turn into a rancid, sticky layer that must be scrubbed off before the wok can be used again.

Hot Fire

Creating great-tasting wok food requires the perfect pan and intense heat. On the highest setting, American gas and electric stoves designed for home use generate about 12,000 BTUs of heat, whereas commercial American restaurant stoves produce up to 18,000 BTUs. In fact, your favorite Chinese restaurant chef stir-fries food in a wok balanced over a "wok jet burner" that produces 150,000 BTUs! It's because of this drastic difference in heat that all wok recipes specify limiting the size of the wok to one no larger than 16 inches in diameter and stir-frying no more than 1 pound of meat or seafood, or 4 cups of vegetables. Both home and commercial stoves do not generate enough heat to maintain the intense temperatures necessary for larger woks or to sear greater amounts of food.

For home cooks who want to duplicate the intense fire used in Chinese restaurants, there are a number of possibilities. Several stove manufacturers, such as Thermador and Gaggenau, manufacture a separate wok burner that produces between 17,500 and 30,000 BTUs. Dacor offers an electric drop-in heating unit shaped like a bowl, which cradles a round-bottom wok. Chinese restaurant-equipment manufacturers produce a variety of free-standing, single-unit wok burners that generate between 70,000 and 150,000 BTUs, and can be modified to fit in an outdoor or indoor cookline counter. Brand names vary across the country, so you will have to check directly with Chinese restaurant suppliers listed in the yellow pages for major cities. In addition, some Asian markets sell portable single-unit wok stoves that generate 50,000 BTUs and can be connected to a propane tank or to an outdoor gas outlet. Finally, for the *Hot Wok* master unable to locate these stoves, simply buying a 24-inch diameter wok at an Asian market and positioning it over an outdoor barbecue will produce fantastic *Hot Wok* dishes. Nestled in a huge bed of coals, the blisteringly hot surface plays host to bold, delectable dishes that are created while guests gather to watch your new outdoor activity.

S *tir-frying involves completing a number of sequential and rhythmic cooking steps in just minutes, using a searingly hot pan. A slight deviation in timing or heating, or a momentary distraction, can affect the quality of wok food. Even if neighbors already proclaim you a Wok Master, reviewing the following basic stir-fry principles may provide a new perspective and enhance your next wok masterpiece.*

Hot Fire, Hot Wok, Hot Action

Hot Wok Preparation

1. Always cut the food, whether meat, seafood, or vegetables, into smaller pieces than you think is necessary. The smaller the food is cut, the faster it cooks and the better it tastes.

2. Cut meat, seafood, and vegetables for a recipe into nearly identical sizes and shapes. This makes it easier while stir-frying to integrate all the ingredients and allows them to cook in similar times.

3. Finish all preparation before beginning the sequential, rhythmic steps of stir-frying. **Advance preparation steps for all recipes can be completed up to 12 hours before stir-frying.**

4. Never cook more than 1 pound of meat or seafood or 4 to 5 cups of vegetables for a wok stir-fry. Attempting to stir-fry a greater amount on a made-for-home or commercial stove, will yield "wok stew." We have found all the meat and seafood stir-fry recipes just as satisfying when using far less meat or seafood than the recipes specify. If you double a recipe, enlist a cooking companion to stir-fry the second portion in another wok.

5. Place the ingredients next to the wok, and line them up in the order they will be added to the wok. Then close the cookbook, or write brief cooking notes on a large sheet of paper and post it next to the wok. Reading recipe directions and cooking in a hot wok are incompatible activities.

Hot Wok Heating

1. For gas and electric stoves, preheat a wok, with no oil in it, for 10 minutes over medium heat until evenly heated and fiery hot. Tap the top inside surface of the wok with your finger to test how hot the wok has become.

2. Having preheated the wok, turn the heat to the highest setting. Always stir-fry over the highest heat, even on a commercial stove. Never reduce the heat throughout the stir-fry process.

Hot Wok Oil

1. For all stir-fry dishes, always use an oil that has a very high smoking point such as peanut or canola oil (referred to as "cooking oil" throughout this book).

2. When beginning to stir-fry, quickly add 1 or 2 tablespoons of cooking oil to the center of the preheated wok. Immediately pick up the wok and roll the oil around its sides. Adding the oil slowly to the center, or pouring the oil down the sides of the wok, will cause the oil to quickly overheat, smoke heavily, and then ignite. If flames occur, cover with a lid, then cool, clean, and reheat the wok.

3. When the oil gives off a wisp of smoke, add the first ingredients.

Hot Wok Stir-Fry

1. To avoid splattering oil, drain the meat or seafood of excess marinade, and completely dry all the vegetables. Place the container holding the prepared food close to the wok's surface, and gently slide the food into the wok.

2. Once the food enters the wok, stir and toss it with a flat wooden spatula. While one hand holds the wok handle, the other stirs, lifts, and turns over the food. Spread the ingredients across the surface in order to sear the food, wait just seconds, and then stir and toss the food again.

3. To properly judge the cooking time, proceed to the next step whenever meat, seafood, vegetables or the Hot Wok Seasonings change color (when meat or seafood loses its raw color, ginger and garlic turn white, or vegetables brighten).

4. To prevent the Hot Wok Seasonings from burning, add the next ingredient almost immediately. This disperses the seasonings and lowers the surface temperature slightly.

5. Undercook everything. The ingredients continue to cook after you've removed them from the hot wok.

Hot Wok Finishing Touches

1. Stir-fry dishes with watery sauces look unattractive and have poor flavor. Although all the Hot Wok Sauces in this book contain a little cornstarch to thicken them, **always prepare 1 extra tablespoon of cornstarch dissolved in 1 tablespoon of cold water.** If at the end of the stir-fry process the sauce appears watery, stir in just enough of this cornstarch mixture to the wok to thicken the sauce and glaze the food.

2. As a final stir-fry step, always taste the dish and adjust the seasonings if necessary.

3. Sliding a stir-fry dish out of a hot, heavy wok is awkward. Always use a wok with two handles. Give the wok a vigorous shake to loosen any food, grab the wok by both handles, and immediately tip the wok toward you (never away from you) so the food slides onto a platter with minimal effort.

4. Serve the dish immediately. Stir-fry dishes never wait for anyone.

How to wok cook seafood so that it retains the essence of the ocean when glazed with complex-flavored sauces

A HOT WOK CAPTURES...

Wok Magic with Seafood

A hot wok captures the natural flavor of shrimp without toughening the exterior, sears fresh scallops so none of their precious moisture escapes, causes small clams and mussels to pop open almost instantly, flash-cooks fresh squid so all the essential sweetness springs forth with each bite, and perfectly cooks thin slices of firm-fleshed fish so the special ocean flavor remains trapped inside.

To wok cook seafood requires good timing and the completion of multiple cooking stages in a few action-filled minutes. Clams and mussels steam open in the wok, then temporarily rest in a bowl before returning to the wok for a noisy, clattering toss with the stir-fry sauce. Barely steamed lobster meat, quickly removed from the shell, sliced, and gently folded into a stir-fry of garden vegetables, delights the palate. Tiny pale squid steaks and purplish tentacles, blanched in boiling water for just a few seconds, curl into twisted rings during the final minutes in the wok. Even a simple stir-fry of thinly sliced fresh sea scallops or tiger prawns wok cooked with minced ginger and a finishing splash of a Hot Wok Sauce, requires careful timing to achieve the ideal balance of flavors.

Key Hot Wok Techniques with Seafood

- Choose fresh raw ocean shrimp, or frozen raw freshwater shrimp, often called "tiger prawns" and most frequently from Thailand, that number 16-20 per pound. Always use fresh scallops, whether they are large sea scallops or small bay scallops. If fresh squid is unavailable, purchase small frozen squid, which will have lost some of the intensely sweet taste. Finally, make no compromises—only buy the very freshest fish. Choose firm-fleshed fish such as tuna, swordfish, and shark, so that the pieces maintain their shape throughout the stir-fry process.

- Few of the seafood recipes use a marinade. Marinating shrimp, scallops, and squid, which have a nonporous exterior, will cause the seafood to steam and the wok oil to splatter. Although firm-fleshed fish are a little more absorbent, use no more than a total of 2 tablespoons liquid marinade (soy, rice wine, and dark sesame oil, for example) per 1 pound of fish.

Don't get stuck in a cooking rut by serving stir-fry dishes only as entrées. Stir-fries, with their complex flavors and brief cooking times, make terrific appetizers. To create your own stir-fry appetizer, just finely dice all the ingredients in your favorite stir-fry dish, prepare, and then serve in endive cups, small Bibb lettuce leaves, or iceberg lettuce cut into neat circles. Accompany the dish with appetizer plates to capture any stray morsels. Guests' expectations for further gastronomic triumphs will be greatly heightened.

Tangerine Shrimp in Endive Cups

SERVES 6 TO 10 AS AN APPETIZER OR 2 AS THE MAIN ENTRÉE

HOT WOK INGREDIENTS

½ pound medium-sized raw shrimp

1 small red bell pepper

2 whole green onions

¼ cup pine nuts

2 heads Belgian endive

2 tablespoons cooking oil

HOT WOK SEASONINGS

2 cloves garlic, finely minced

1 teaspoon finely minced tangerine or orange zest

HOT WOK SAUCE

¼ cup tangerine or orange juice, freshly squeezed

1 tablespoon fish sauce

2 teaspoons hoisin sauce

1 teaspoon Asian chile sauce

2 teaspoons cornstarch

¼ cup shredded mint leaves

3 tablespoons chopped cilantro

ADVANCE PREPARATION

Preheat the oven to 325°. Shell and devein the shrimp. Cut the shrimp crosswise into ¼-inch-wide pieces and refrigerate. Discard stem and seeds from the pepper. Cut the pepper into ¼-inch-wide strips, then cut across strips to make ¼-inch cubes. Cut the green onions on a sharp diagonal into ¼-inch-wide pieces, combine with the pepper, and refrigerate. Toast pine nuts in the preheated oven until golden, about 8 minutes, and reserve. Cut ends off endive, separate the leaves, and refrigerate. In a small container, set aside the cooking oil.

In a small container, combine the Hot Wok Seasonings; set aside. In a small bowl, combine the Hot Wok Sauce ingredients, and refrigerate.

HOT WOK ACTION

Place a wok over the highest heat. When the wok is very hot, add the cooking oil to the center. Roll the oil around the sides of the wok and add the Hot Wok Seasonings. When seasonings just begin to turn white, in about 5 seconds, add the shrimp. Stir-fry just until the shrimp lose their raw exterior color, about 30 seconds.

Stir in the pepper and green onions. Stir and toss the vegetables until they brighten in color, about 15 seconds, then add the Hot Wok Sauce. Stir-fry until the sauce thickens and glazes the shrimp, about 15 seconds. Stir in the pine nuts, then taste and adjust the seasonings. Slide the stir-fry out of the wok onto a heated serving platter. Surround with endive cups and serve at once.

Chinese restaurants tenderize raw shrimp by marinating them in egg whites, a process called "velveting." Because the marinade would stick to the sides of the wok, the velveted shrimp are poached in oil, drained, and then returned to the wok to be quickly stir-fried with the vegetables. For nearly all home-style shrimp stir-fry dishes, we find the end results just as satisfying when we omit the marinade and stir-fry the shrimp rather than poaching them in oil. In this recipe, however, velveting and poaching the shrimp makes them especially beautiful when glazed with the clear lemon sauce. If you don't wish to use the velveting-poaching technique, just stir-fry the shrimp as described in the other stir-fry shrimp recipes.

Sizzling Lemon Shrimp on Puff Pastry

SERVES 4 AS THE MAIN ENTRÉE

HOT WOK INGREDIENTS

1 pound medium-sized raw shrimp

2 egg whites

1 tablespoon rice wine or dry sherry

1 tablespoon cornstarch

¼ teaspoon salt

⅛ teaspoon finely ground white pepper

1 6x6-inch square of frozen puff pastry

1 bunch chives

2 cups cooking oil

HOT WOK SAUCE

1 tablespoon very finely minced fresh
    ginger

2 teaspoons finely minced lemon zest

½ cup lemon juice, freshly squeezed

6 tablespoons sugar

¼ cup chicken stock

2 tablespoons thin soy sauce

1 tablespoon cornstarch

½ teaspoon salt

ADVANCE PREPARATION

Shell, devein, and split the shrimp deeply lengthwise. In a small bowl, combine the egg whites, rice wine, cornstarch, salt, and pepper. Add the shrimp and mix thoroughly with your fingers. Refrigerate the shrimp at least 30 minutes but not longer than 8 hours.

Cut the sheet of puff pastry into 4 3x3-inch squares (or other shapes) and refrigerate, covered. Chop the chives. Set aside the cooking oil. In a small nonreactive saucepan combine the ingredients for the Hot Wok Sauce, mix well, and refrigerate.

HOT WOK ACTION

Preheat the oven to 450°. Place the puff pastry on a baking sheet, and bake in the preheated oven until golden and puffed, about 15 minutes.

Place saucepan containing the Hot Wok Sauce over medium heat, bring to a low boil, and cook until the lemon sauce thickens, about 1 minute. Then reduce heat to the lowest setting and keep hot.

Place a colander over a heat-proof bowl or saucepan. Place a wok over the highest heat. When the wok becomes very hot, add the cooking oil. As soon as tiny bubbles form when the tip of a wooden spoon is dipped into the oil, add the shrimp. Gently stir and toss the shrimp. When the shrimp turn white and have lost their raw interior color (cut into a shrimp to check for doneness), immediately slide the shrimp into the colander to drain.

Place the puff pastry squares on 4 heated dinner plates. Place the shrimp on the puff pastry, spoon the lemon sauce over the top of them, sprinkle on the chopped chives, and serve at once.

This Asian "pesto," which is a combination of various Asian herbs and spices puréed in an electric blender, adds an alluring range of flavors and a startling jade color when tossed with the shrimp in a hot wok. Try substituting large sea scallops cut into thin slices, or fresh squid cleaned according to the directions on page 26, for the shrimp. Or take a night off from stir-frying and toss 1 pound of fresh ravioli, boiled and drained, with the sauce and a grating of imported Parmesan.

Jade Shrimp with Mint, Basil, Cilantro, and Chiles

SERVES 4 AS THE MAIN ENTRÉE

HOT WOK INGREDIENTS

1 pound medium-sized raw shrimp

½ red bell pepper

1 tablespoon white sesame seeds

2 tablespoons cooking oil

HOT WOK SEASONINGS

3 cloves garlic, finely minced

1 tablespoon very finely minced fresh ginger

HOT WOK SAUCE

1 cup spinach leaves

¼ cup mint leaves

¼ cup cilantro sprigs

10 large basil leaves

1 small green onion, green ends only, chopped

2 tablespoons rice wine or dry sherry

2 tablespoons dark sesame oil

1 tablespoon thin soy sauce

1 teaspoon cornstarch

2 teaspoons hoisin sauce

2 teaspoons sugar

1 teaspoon Asian chile sauce

1 teaspoon finely minced orange zest

ADVANCE PREPARATION

Shell, devein, and split each shrimp in half lengthwise; then refrigerate. Stem, seed, and dice red pepper. Place the sesame seeds in a small ungreased skillet, and sauté over medium heat until they turn light golden. Immediately remove the sesame seeds from the skillet, and set aside. In a small container, set aside the cooking oil.

In a small bowl, combine the Hot Wok Seasonings; set aside. To prepare the Hot Wok Sauce, place all sauce ingredients in an electric blender, and blend into a smooth liquid. The sauce can be prepared up to 8 hours in advance if refrigerated until used.

HOT WOK ACTION

Place a wok over the highest heat. When the wok becomes very hot, add the cooking oil to the center. Roll the oil around the wok and when the oil gives off just a wisp of smoke, add the Hot Wok Seasonings. Stir-fry the seasonings, and as soon as they turn white, about 5 seconds, add the shrimp. Stir and toss the shrimp until their exteriors turn white, about 2 minutes.

Stir the Hot Wok Sauce, and then pour it into the wok. Stir and toss until the shrimp are glazed with the sauce and are cooked through, about 1 minute. Taste and adjust the seasonings. Immediately transfer the stir-fry onto a heated dinner platter or dinner plates. Sprinkle on the diced red peppers and toasted sesame seeds and serve at once.

For all shrimp stir-fry dishes we prefer freshwater shrimp, which have no vein and are not processed with the distasteful iodine-like preservative found in many ocean shrimp. Deeply butterflied or split in half lengthwise, shrimp this size take little time to shell, and look exquisite stir-fried. The special ingredient in this recipe, black bean sauce, is made from black beans that are salted, fermented, and then mashed into a paste with garlic, vinegar, and sugar. The sauce's deep, low-note flavor blends with nutty, dark sesame oil and creates a dynamic contrast with the spicy high notes of fresh serrano chiles.

Spicy Shrimp in Hunan Black Bean Sauce

SERVES 4 AS THE MAIN ENTRÉE

HOT WOK INGREDIENTS

1 pound medium-sized raw shrimp

1 red bell pepper

1 green bell pepper

1 yellow bell pepper

3 tablespoons cooking oil

dash of dark sesame oil

salt and freshly ground black pepper, to taste

HOT WOK SEASONINGS

4 cloves garlic, finely minced

1 large shallot, finely minced

1 tablespoon finely minced fresh ginger

3 fresh serrano chiles, including seeds, finely minced

HOT WOK SAUCE

¼ cup rice wine or dry sherry

1 tablespoon thin soy sauce

1 tablespoon dark sesame oil

1 tablespoon black bean sauce

1 tablespoon red wine vinegar

1 tablespoon sugar

2 teaspoons cornstarch

ADVANCE PREPARATION

Shell, devein, and split each shrimp in half lengthwise; then refrigerate. Discard the stems and seeds from the peppers. Cut the peppers into matchstick pieces about 1 inch long and ¼ inch wide. Combine all the peppers and set aside, refrigerated. Divide the cooking oil in half and set aside. Set aside the dash of sesame oil, and the salt and pepper.

In a small container, combine the Hot Wok Seasonings; set aside. In a small bowl, combine the Hot Wok Sauce ingredients; set aside.

HOT WOK ACTION

Preheat the oven to 200°. Place a wok over the highest heat. When the wok becomes very hot, add 1½ tablespoons of the cooking oil to the center. Roll the oil around the wok and when the oil gives off just a wisp of smoke, add the peppers. Stir and toss the peppers until they brighten in color, about 2 minutes. During the final seconds of cooking, add the sesame oil, salt, and pepper. Immediately slide the peppers onto a heated platter or dinner plates, spreading them in an even layer, and place in the oven.

Immediately return the wok to the highest heat. Add the remaining cooking oil to the wok. Roll the oil around the sides of the wok and when the oil gives off just a wisp of smoke, add the Hot Wok Seasonings. Stir-fry the seasonings, and as soon as they turn white, about 5 seconds, add the shrimp. Stir and toss the shrimp until their exteriors turn white, about 2 minutes.

Stir the Hot Wok Sauce, and then pour the sauce into the wok. Stir and toss until the shrimp are glazed with the sauce and cooked through, about 1 minute. Taste and adjust the seasonings. Immediately spoon the shrimp into the center of the stir-fried peppers and serve at once.

ry fry means stir-frying shrimp in a blisteringly hot wok without the addition of any cooking oil or sauce. The preparation involves simply cutting along the top ridge of the shrimp shells, packing a marinade under the shells, and then cooking the shrimp in the wok until the shells begin to blister and the shrimp feel firm to the touch. The shells shield the shrimp meat, capture the marinade, and intensify the shrimp taste. Delicious hot or chilled, this dish does require a little hands-on effort when slipping the dry-fried shrimp out of their shells.

Szechwan Dry-Fried Shrimp

SERVES 4 AS THE MAIN ENTRÉE

HOT WOK INGREDIENTS

1 pound large raw shrimp, shells on

3 limes

HOT WOK SEASONINGS

6 cloves garlic, finely minced

3 tablespoons very finely minced fresh ginger

2 shallots, finely minced

3 whole green onions, minced

2 tablespoons oyster sauce

3 tablespoons rice wine or dry sherry

1 tablespoon Asian chile sauce

1 tablespoon dark sesame oil

1 tablespoon cooking oil

1 tablespoon brown sugar

ADVANCE PREPARATION

Using scissors, clip along the top of the shrimp shells. Then without removing the shell, cut along the top ridge of each shrimp and rinse away the vein. Cut the limes into wedges; set aside.

In a small bowl, combine the Hot Wok Seasonings. Gently pack the seasonings under the shrimp shells. Marinate the shrimp at least 15 minutes but not longer than 8 hours, refrigerated.

HOT WOK ACTION

Place a wok over the highest heat. When the wok becomes very hot, add the shrimp. Dry-fry the shrimp by stirring and tossing them until their shells begin to blacken. The shrimp are cooked when they feel firm to the touch, about 2 minutes. Immediately transfer the shrimp to a heated serving platter or dinner plates and serve at once with lime wedges.

This gastronomic attack, with its waves of chiles, citrus, garlic, and vinegar glazing the tender scallops, and with crisp toasted peanuts and brightly colored peppers, increases in volatility until bowls of sticky rice, pitchers of Tsing Tao beer, and iced terry cloth towels have no cooling effect as eyelids perspire and tongues curl. Hands tremble while reaching for further helpings and the Chinese chile zone of pleasure arrives.

Kung Pow with Fresh Bay Scallops

SERVES 4 AS THE MAIN ENTRÉE

HOT WOK INGREDIENTS

1 pound fresh bay scallops

2 cups cherry tomatoes

4 whole green onions

1 cup raw peanuts, shelled and skinned

1 cup cooking oil

HOT WOK SEASONINGS

4 cloves garlic, finely minced

1 tablespoon very finely minced fresh ginger

HOT WOK SAUCE

⅓ cup orange juice, freshly squeezed

¼ cup rice wine or dry sherry

2 tablespoons oyster sauce

1 tablespoon hoisin sauce

1 tablespoon dark sesame oil

1 tablespoon red wine vinegar

1 tablespoon cornstarch

1 teaspoon Asian chile sauce

¼ teaspoon ground Szechwan peppercorns

⅓ cup seeded small whole dried red chiles

ADVANCE PREPARATION

Place the scallops in a small bowl and refrigerate. Discard the tomato stems. Cut the green onions on a sharp diagonal into 1-inch lengths. In a bowl, combine the vegetables and refrigerate.

In a small saucepan, combine peanuts and the cooking oil. Place the saucepan over medium heat. Stir the peanuts slowly, and when they turn light golden, about 4 minutes, immediately transfer the nuts and oil to a strainer placed over a heat-proof container. Set aside the nuts at room temperature. Reserve 3 tablespoons of the cooking oil, divided, for stir-frying.

In a small bowl, combine the Hot Wok Seasonings; set aside. In another small bowl, combine the Hot Wok Sauce ingredients. Stir well and refrigerate.

HOT WOK ACTION

Place a wok over the highest heat. When the wok becomes very hot, add half the reserved cooking oil to the center. Roll the oil around the wok and when the oil gives off just a wisp of smoke, add the scallops. Stir and toss the scallops until they lose their raw exterior color, about 1 minute, then slide the scallops onto a plate.

Immediately return the wok to the highest heat. Add the remaining cooking oil, and the Hot Wok Seasonings. Stir-fry the seasonings, and as soon as they turn white, about 5 seconds, add the vegetables. Stir and toss the vegetables until the green onions brighten in color, about 2 minutes.

Stir the Hot Wok Sauce, and then pour it into the wok. Return the scallops to the wok and add the peanuts. Stir and toss until all the ingredients are glazed with the sauce. Taste and adjust the seasonings. Immediately transfer the stir-fry to a heated platter or dinner plates and serve.

Frozen, thawed scallops expel a milky liquid the instant they touch the sides of a hot wok, so always examine scallops carefully before buying. Fresh scallops have some clear liquid surrounding them and a distinct fresh scallop smell. Frozen, thawed scallops have no smell and usually sit in a puddle of milky liquid. For the following recipe, if large fresh sea scallops are not available, substitute small fresh bay scallops and cut the snow peas in half on the diagonal.

Chile-Tangerine Scallops

SERVES 4 AS THE MAIN ENTRÉE

HOT WOK INGREDIENTS

1 pound fresh sea scallops

2 cups small snow peas

1 large red onion

3 tablespoons cooking oil

HOT WOK SEASONINGS

6 cloves garlic, finely minced

1 tablespoon very finely minced fresh
    ginger

2 fresh serrano chiles, including seeds,
    finely minced

HOT WOK SAUCE

2 teaspoons finely minced tangerine
    zest

⅓ cup tangerine juice, freshly squeezed

2 tablespoons rice wine or dry sherry

1 tablespoon hoisin sauce

1 tablespoon cornstarch

1 tablespoon dark sesame oil

2 teaspoons red wine vinegar

1 teaspoon sugar

½ teaspoon finely ground Szechwan
    pepper

ADVANCE PREPARATION

Cut each scallop into 3 or 4 thin slices and refrigerate. Snap off and discard the stem ends of the snow peas. Peel the onion, cut into 8 wedges, and then cut each wedge in half. Combine the vegetables, and refrigerate. Divide the cooking oil in half and set aside.

In a small bowl, combine the Hot Wok Seasonings; set aside. In another small bowl, combine the Hot Wok Sauce ingredients. Stir well and refrigerate.

HOT WOK ACTION

Place a wok over the highest heat. When the wok becomes very hot, add half the cooking oil to the center. Roll the oil around the wok and when the oil gives off just a wisp of smoke, add the scallops. Stir and toss the scallops until they lose their raw exterior color, about 1 minute. Immediately slide the scallops onto a plate.

Immediately return the wok to the highest heat. Add the remaining cooking oil, and the Hot Wok Seasonings. Stir-fry the seasonings, and as soon as they turn white, about 5 seconds, add the vegetables. Stir and toss the vegetables until the onion separates into layers and the snow peas brighten in color, about 2 minutes.

Stir the Hot Wok Sauce, and then pour it into the wok. Return the scallops to the wok. Stir and toss until all the ingredients are glazed with the sauce. Taste and adjust the seasonings. Immediately transfer the stir-fry to a heated platter or dinner plates and serve.

*M*ussels and clams taste wonderful glazed with any of the sauces in this book. Just steam open in a saucepan containing 1 inch of boiling water, then transfer the mussels or clams to a colander. In a wok, sauté the Hot Wok Seasonings in a little cooking oil, pour in the Hot Wok Sauce, and after it thickens, add the mussels or clams in their shells. Complete the cooking by sprinkling the wok's contents with fresh herbs, such as chopped cilantro, basil, or mint, and stirring vigorously until everything becomes glazed with the sauce. The following recipe uses a Thai "curry" paste of chiles and fresh herbs, which tastes very different than the Indian curry powders and pastes.

Green Curry Mussels

SERVES 4 AS THE MAIN ENTRÉE

HOT WOK INGREDIENTS

32 small black mussels
1 red bell pepper
2 cups water

HOT WOK SEASONINGS

3 tablespoons cooking oil
4 cloves garlic, minced
1 tablespoon minced fresh ginger
1 small shallot, minced
4 fresh serrano chiles, including seeds, minced

HOT WOK SAUCE

1 cup loosely packed basil leaves, chopped
½ cup loosely packed cilantro sprigs, chopped
6 fresh serrano chiles, including seeds, chopped
1 cup coconut milk
¼ cup rice wine or dry sherry
2 tablespoons fish sauce
2 tablespoons brown sugar
1 teaspoon ground coriander
½ teaspoon ground caraway

ADVANCE PREPARATION

If any of the mussels are open within 4 hours before cooking, cover them with cold water for 5 minutes. Then drain away the water and discard any mussels that have not closed. Scrub the mussels, pulling away any seaweed between the shell halves. Refrigerate the mussels until ready to cook.

Discard stem and seeds from the bell pepper. Chop the pepper into ¼-inch pieces and set aside. Set aside the water. In a small bowl combine the Hot Wok Seasonings; set aside. In another small bowl combine the Hot Wok Sauce ingredients; set aside, refrigerated.

HOT WOK ACTION

Place a wok over the highest heat. Add the water, and when it comes to a vigorous boil, add the mussels and cover the wok tightly. Steam the mussels until they open, about 4 minutes. Immediately slide the mussels into a colander. Discard any mussels that have not opened.

Return the wok to the highest heat. Add the Hot Wok Seasonings and when the garlic sizzles, about 1 minute, add the Hot Wok Sauce. Bring the sauce to a vigorous boil. Then return the mussels to the wok, and stir them gently until they are completely glazed with the sauce. Taste and adjust the seasonings. Stir in the bell pepper. Immediately transfer the stir-fry to a heated platter or dinner plates and serve.

All the recipes in this book are designed to serve 4 people. As already explained, standard American home stoves and commercial ranges only generate enough heat to properly sear the quantities of ingredients listed in these recipes. If you want to double a recipe, but wish to avoid making "wok soup," then enlist the aid of a friend to simultaneously stir-fry the same dish in a neighboring wok. Make a single stir-fry dish the gastronomic feature of a menu and control the impulse to include more than one Hot Wok recipe. Without the help of a staff, multiple stir-fry courses quickly degenerate into a wok nightmare as the increasingly weary cook dashes maniacally from table to stove while the guests feel ignored and the magic of the evening dissipates.

Hot Wok Menu Planning and Presentation

Use *Hot Wok* recipes as a starting point for workday dinners or weekend parties. For example, begin with stir-fried Tangerine Shrimp in Endive Cups (page 9) as an appetizer, followed by a hearty stew and a Caesar salad. Or start the festivities with a home-cured Gravlax, then as the entrée, serve stir-fried Thai Duck with Cilantro, Chiles, and Garlic (page 43) with wild rice, followed by a walnut-spinach salad and a rich chocolate tart. Or stir-fry Tricolor Fusilli with Wild Mushrooms (page 84) as a simple late-night vegetarian dinner.

What starch should you serve with Hot Wok entrées? Just follow the two-thousand-year-old Asian tradition of preparing steamed white rice or boiled noodles (instructions for steaming rice appear on page 97). Or, break out of the Chinese-menu rut and serve Hot Wok dishes with wild rice, bulgur wheat, garlic bread, sour dough rolls, polenta, couscous, corn bread, or one of the following suggestions.

Accompany with Lettuce Cups: Serving a piping-hot stir-fry inside a cool, crisp lettuce wrapping creates a wonderful textural contrast. Cut off the choke end from a head of iceberg lettuce, then carefully remove the leaves and trim the edges to make cups. Or use the small interior leaves from Bibb or romaine lettuce. Or, if all the stir-fry ingredients have been cut into a fine dice, accompany the stir-fry with large green- and red-leaf endive cups.

Wrap in Soft Chinese Tacos: Hot Chinese or Mexican wrappers, or Middle Eastern pita pockets, make excellent shells to fill with stir-fried food. Seal a stack of Chinese mu shu wrappers, Mexican flour or corn tortillas, or pita bread in foil and warm them in a 325° oven for 15 minutes. Alternatively, place the wrapper directly on a gas stove-top flame to warm (about 5 seconds on each side), or warm in the microwave oven. Accompany the wrappers with the stir-fry dish, and one or more condiments such as hoisin sauce, plum sauce, Dijon-style mustard, or salsa. When cooking the stir-fry, limit the amount of the Hot Wok Sauce to no more than 6 tablespoons so that the stir-fry does not make the wrapper soggy.

Serve on Crisp Rice Sticks: Crisp, intensely white Chinese rice sticks make a great foundation on top of which to position a stir-fry dish. Place 2 ounces of rice sticks in a paper bag and pull apart into small bundles. Add 1 inch of cooking oil to a 10-inch frying pan, and place the frying pan over medium heat. Heat the oil until a strand puffs up immediately when added to the oil. Add the rice sticks a few at a time, and when they expand (within 3 seconds), using tongs, turn the rice sticks over and push them momentarily back into the oil. Immediately remove the rice sticks from the oil and drain on paper towels. Store the cooked rice sticks in a paper bag at room temperature no longer than 6 hours. To use: just before beginning to cook the stir-fry, break the rice sticks into 2-inch lengths, and spread across the surface of a platter.

Use Crisp Pan-Fried Noodles as a Foundation: Crisp pan-fried noodle "pillows," soft in the center but crunchy on the outside, also provide dramatic textural contrast when served with stir-fries. Be sure to double the Hot Wok Sauce so there is plenty to saturate the noodles. Boil ½ pound dried spaghetti-style noodles in 5 quarts of lightly salted water, and drain the noodles when they are barely cooked in the center. Rinse briefly with cold water, drain thoroughly, and then spread the noodles evenly across the surface of a 12-inch lightly oiled plate. Dry the noodles, uncovered, at room temperature for 4 to 8 hours. Just prior to stir-frying, preheat an oven to 200°. Place a 12- or 14-inch cast-iron skillet over medium heat, and when very hot, add ¼ cup of cooking oil. When the oil becomes hot, gently transfer the noodle "pillow" to the pan. Pan-fry the noodles about 5 minutes on each side, until both sides turn golden. Remove from the frying pan, cut the noodles into wedges, transfer the noodles to a serving platter, and keep warm in the preheated oven. Complete the stir-fry, position the stir-fry on top of the noodles, and serve at once.

Make Polenta the Base: Cut into stars, wedges, or triangles, with each piece having a crisp exterior and soft, creamy interior, polenta makes an innovative foundation for stir-fry dishes. In a 2½ quart saucepan, combine 2 cups yellow cornmeal, 6 cups of cold water, and 2 teaspoons salt. Place the saucepan over medium heat, bring the water to a low boil, and as the polenta begins to thicken, reduce the heat to low. Stir the polenta slowly, but continually, until it becomes so thick it begins to pull away from the sides of the saucepan, about 15 minutes from the time the water comes to a low boil. Stir in ½ cup butter, cut into small pieces, and ½ cup freshly grated, imported Parmesan cheese. Immediately spoon the polenta onto a baking sheet, and spread it into a ½-inch-thick layer. Let cool at room temperature at least 1 hour. This can be done a day in advance and refrigerated. Just before stir-frying, preheat the oven to broil. Cut the polenta into stars, rectangles, squares or other shapes. Brush the top of the polenta with extra virgin olive oil, and place the baking sheet 4 inches below the broiler heat. Broil the polenta until golden, about 8 minutes. Arrange the polenta on a heated platter or on individual serving plates. Position the stir-fry in the center of the polenta and serve at once.

During soft-shell crab season, which lasts from spring to early fall, millions of small blue crabs shed their hard shells. During the few days it takes for a new exoskeleton to form, these crabs become a culinary prize to small and large predators. Only buy soft-shell crabs that are alive. Ask the market to clean them for you and, because they are highly perishable, cook them the same day you buy them. The entire crab is edible. Try substituting soft-shell crabs in any shrimp or scallop stir-fry. Leave the soft-shell crabs whole for a dramatic visual presentation, or if using chopsticks, cut the crabs into quarters just before you put them in the wok.

Soft-Shell Crab Bonanza

SERVES 4 AS THE MAIN ENTRÉE

HOT WOK INGREDIENTS

6 fresh soft-shell crabs, cleaned

3 whole green onions

8 stalks asparagus

3 tablespoons cooking oil

HOT WOK SEASONING

2 cloves garlic, finely minced

HOT WOK SAUCE

⅔ cup chicken stock

2 tablespoons tomato sauce

2 tablespoons oyster sauce

2 tablespoons rice wine or dry sherry

1 tablespoon thin soy sauce

1 tablespoon dark sesame oil

1 tablespoon cornstarch

½ teaspoon sugar

¼ teaspoon freshly ground black pepper

ADVANCE PREPARATION

Set aside whole crabs, or cut in half or quarters. Cut the green onions on a sharp diagonal into 1-inch-long pieces. Snap off and discard tough asparagus stems. Cut the asparagus on a sharp diagonal into 1-inch-long pieces. Place the asparagus in a single layer on a dinner plate, cover with plastic wrap, and microwave on high for 1 minute at a time, until the asparagus brighten in color. Or, stir the asparagus into 2 quarts of boiling water. As soon as the asparagus brighten in color, about 1 minute, immediately transfer them to a colander, then to a bowl filled with cold water and ice. When the asparagus are chilled, drain them and pat dry with paper towels. In a bowl, combine the green onions and asparagus, then refrigerate. Divide the cooking oil in half and set aside.

In a small bowl, set aside the garlic. In another small bowl, combine the Hot Wok Sauce ingredients. Stir well and refrigerate.

HOT WOK ACTION

Place a wok over the highest heat. When the wok becomes very hot, add half the cooking oil to the center. Roll the oil around the wok and when the oil gives off just a wisp of smoke, add the soft-shell crabs. Stir and toss the crabs until they turn red on the outside, about 3 minutes, then slide them onto a plate.

Immediately return the wok to the highest heat. Add the remaining cooking oil, and the garlic. Stir-fry the garlic, and as soon as it turns white, about 5 seconds, add the vegetables. Stir and toss the vegetables until the green onions brighten in color, about 2 minutes.

Stir the Hot Wok Sauce, and then pour it into the wok. Return the crab to the wok. Stir and toss until all the ingredients are glazed with the sauce. Taste and adjust the seasonings. Immediately transfer the stir-fry to a heated platter or dinner plates and serve.

Homemade salsas, with their sparkle of fresh flavors, add a wonderful element to stir-fry dishes. Either serve the room-temperature salsa in a decorative bowl to be spooned across stir-fried meat or seafood, or substitute your favorite salsa for the Hot Wok Sauce in any stir-fry recipe. When you add the salsa to the wok, stir in a little cornstarch thickener (an equal amount of cornstarch and cold water stirred together) so the salsa ingredients glaze the food during the final seconds of stir-frying. Black sesame seeds, the garnish in this recipe, are available at all Asian markets.

Squid with Hawaiian Mango Salsa

SERVES 6 TO 10 AS AN APPETIZER OR 4 AS THE MAIN ENTRÉE

HOT WOK INGREDIENTS

1 pound small fresh squid

1 bunch chives, chopped

2 tablespoons cooking oil

1 tablespoon black sesame seeds

HOT WOK SEASONING

2 tablespoons very finely minced fresh
    ginger

HOT WOK SAUCE

3 tablespoons rice wine or dry sherry

1 tablespoon oyster sauce

1 teaspoon cornstarch

HAWAIIAN MANGO SALSA

2 ripe mangoes

¼ cup chopped mint leaves

¼ cup chopped cilantro

1 whole green onion, minced

1 tablespoon very finely minced fresh
    ginger

2 fresh serrano chiles, including seeds,
    finely minced

3 tablespoons lime juice, freshly
    squeezed

2 tablespoons brown sugar

2 tablespoons fish sauce

ADVANCE PREPARATION

Clean the squid as described in the recipe for Gingered Squid with Sugar Snap Peas (page 26). In separate containers, set aside the chives, cooking oil, and black sesame seeds. Set aside the ginger for seasoning. In a small bowl, combine the Hot Wok Sauce ingredients and set aside.

To make the Hawaiian Salsa, peel the mango and cut away the flesh in large pieces. Coarsely chop the flesh. Then in a medium-sized mixing bowl, combine the mango with the remaining salsa ingredients. Transfer the salsa to a decorative bowl and place in the center of a round platter. Set aside at room temperature.

HOT WOK ACTION

Using paper towels, pat the squid dry after cleaning. Place a wok over the highest heat. When the wok becomes very hot, add the cooking oil to the center. Roll the oil around the wok, and when the oil gives off just a wisp of smoke, add the ginger for seasoning. Stir and toss until the ginger turns white, about 15 seconds. Add the squid. Stir and toss the squid until it loses its raw exterior color, about 1 minute.

Stir the Hot Wok Sauce, and then pour it into the wok. Stir and toss until the squid is glazed with the sauce, about 15 seconds. Immediately spoon the squid around the bowl of mango salsa.

Scatter chopped chives and black sesame seeds over the squid and serve at once. Each person seasons the squid with the Hawaiian Mango Salsa.

European chefs are usually aghast at the combination of delicate, sweet-tasting squid glazed with such assertive Chinese and Thai seasonings as chiles, garlic, and ginger. But as fiery-food devotees know, once addicted to chiles, all the flavors of the most understated ingredients, such as fresh scallops, shrimp, and in this recipe, squid, shine forth.

Gingered Squid with Sugar Snap Peas

SERVES 4 AS THE MAIN ENTRÉE

HOT WOK INGREDIENTS

1 pound small fresh squid

4 small vine-ripened tomatoes

3 whole green onions

4 cups sugar snap peas (about ¼ pound)

1 tablespoon cooking oil

HOT WOK SEASONINGS

¼ pound lean ground pork

8 cloves garlic, finely minced

1 tablespoon very finely minced fresh ginger

HOT WOK SAUCE

¼ cup rice wine or dry sherry

1 tablespoon heavy soy sauce

1 tablespoon dark sesame oil

1 tablespoon Asian chile sauce

2 teaspoons red wine vinegar

2 teaspoons cornstarch

1 teaspoon sugar

¼ teaspoon salt

ADVANCE PREPARATION

Clean the squid by pulling the heads from them and cutting the tentacles off in one piece. If the black mouth is in the center of the tentacles, pull this away and discard. Discard the rest of the head. Under cold running water, rub off the squid skin with your fingers. Run a thin knife inside the squid and cut open into a flat steak. Clean the inside thoroughly. Then make lengthwise cuts ½ inch apart along the inside of the squid steak, being careful not to cut all the way through. Make crosswise cuts ½ inch apart, creating a diamond pattern. Cut each steak into 4 quarters, then refrigerate, along with the tentacles.

Cut the tomatoes in half through the middle. Squeeze out the seeds and cut the tomatoes into thin wedges. Cut the green onions on a sharp diagonal into 1-inch lengths. In a bowl, combine the tomatoes, green onions, and sugar snap peas, then refrigerate. Set aside the cooking oil.

In a small bowl, combine the Hot Wok Seasonings; set aside. In another small bowl, combine the Hot Wok Sauce ingredients; stir well and set aside.

HOT WOK ACTION

In a large pot, bring 4 quarts of water to a vigorous boil. Place a wok over the highest heat. When the wok becomes very hot, add the cooking oil to the center. Roll the oil around the wok and when the oil gives off just a wisp of smoke, add the Hot Wok Seasonings. Stir-fry the seasonings, breaking the ground pork into little pieces until the pork loses all of its pink color, about 2 minutes.

Immediately, add the vegetables. Stir and toss the vegetables until the sugar snap peas brighten in color, about 1 minute.

Stir the squid into the boiling water. As soon as the squid turn white, about 10 seconds, transfer them to a colander to drain, and then immediately add the squid to the wok.

Stir the Hot Wok Sauce, and then pour it into the wok. Stir and toss until all the ingredients are glazed with the sauce. Taste and adjust the seasonings. Immediately transfer the stir-fry to a heated platter or dinner plates and serve.

This recipe reflects a fusion of seasoning and cooking methods from diverse traditions. The key in this type of cross-cultural cooking is to achieve the right balance of seasonings so there are no discordant flavor notes. When creating your own wok dishes, choose as your primary flavors a blend of seasonings and spices that traditionally work well together, and then integrate just a few complementary or contrasting flavor elements from another cuisine. Taste as you add seasonings and err on the side of caution so flavor chaos does not ensue.

Swordfish and Wild Mushrooms with Tarragon and Chiles

SERVES 4 AS THE MAIN ENTRÉE

HOT WOK INGREDIENTS

1 pound fresh swordfish

¼ cup, plus 1 tablespoon rice wine or dry sherry

1 tablespoon thin soy sauce

1 tablespoon dark sesame oil

¼ pound fresh chanterelle mushrooms

¼ pound fresh shiitake mushrooms

¼ pound fresh portabello mushrooms

2 whole green onions

1 cup shelled sweet peas

1 tablespoon fresh tarragon leaves

3 tablespoons cooking oil

HOT WOK SEASONINGS

1 tablespoon very finely minced fresh ginger

1 large shallot, minced

HOT WOK SAUCE

⅓ cup chicken stock

¼ cup rice wine or dry sherry

3 tablespoons tomato sauce

2 tablespoons oyster sauce

1 tablespoon cornstarch

½ teaspoon Asian chile sauce

½ teaspoon salt

ADVANCE PREPARATION

Cut off and discard all swordfish skin. Cut the swordfish into ¼-inch-thick slices. Cut each slice into 1-inch lengths. In a small bowl, combine 1 tablespoon of the rice wine, the soy sauce, and sesame oil, and then mix thoroughly with the swordfish. Marinate the swordfish at least 15 minutes but not longer than 8 hours, refrigerated. Set aside the remaining rice wine.

Trim tough ends from all the mushrooms. Cut the mushrooms into ¼-inch-thick slices. Cut the green onions on a sharp diagonal into 1-inch-long pieces, combine with the mushrooms and peas, and refrigerate. Set aside the tarragon leaves. Divide the cooking oil and set aside.

In a small bowl, combine the Hot Wok Seasonings; set aside. In another small bowl, combine the Hot Wok Sauce ingredients and refrigerate.

HOT WOK ACTION

Place a wok over the highest heat. When the wok becomes very hot, add half the cooking oil to the center. Roll the oil around the wok and when the oil gives off just a wisp of smoke, add the swordfish. Stir and toss the swordfish until it loses its raw exterior color, about 1½ minutes, and slide the swordfish onto a plate.

Immediately return the wok to the highest heat. Add the remaining cooking oil and the Hot Wok Seasonings. Stir-fry the seasonings, and as soon as they turn white, about 5 seconds, add the mushrooms and peas. Stir and toss until the peas brighten in color and the mushrooms soften slightly, about 3 minutes. As you stir-fry the mushrooms, add the remaining rice wine, so that the mushrooms soften more quickly and develop a fuller flavor.

Stir the Hot Wok Sauce, and then pour the sauce into the wok. Add the tarragon and return the swordfish to the wok. Stir and toss until all the ingredients are glazed with the sauce. Taste and adjust the seasonings. Immediately transfer the stir-fry to a heated platter or dinner plates and serve.

It is important that clams and mussels be alive until the moment they are cooked to ensure their freshness. There are a few other rules to follow, too: Only buy those that are closed tightly. Always store clams and mussels refrigerated in a bowl that is loosely covered with a wet cloth or paper towel because keeping them in an airtight container or submerged in cold water causes the bivalves to suffocate. Plan on cooking clams and mussels within 2 days of purchase. Prior to cooking, cover them with cold water. Discard any open bivalves that do not close tightly after 5 minutes in the water. Clams and mussels are thoroughly cooked the moment their shells pop open in the hot wok. Discard any that remain tightly closed during cooking.

Clams Glistening with Asian Salsa

SERVES 4 AS THE MAIN ENTRÉE

HOT WOK INGREDIENTS

40 black steamer clams
2 tablespoons cooking oil
2 cups water

HOT WOK SEASONINGS

5 cloves garlic, finely minced
1 tablespoon very finely minced fresh ginger

HOT WOK SALSA

6 dried Chinese mushrooms
½ cup chopped vine-ripened tomatoes
¼ cup coarsely chopped cilantro
½ cup whole green onions, minced
2 tablespoons oyster sauce
2 tablespoons dark sesame oil
2 teaspoons Asian chile sauce
1 tablespoon dry sherry
2 teaspoons sugar
2 teaspoons cornstarch

ADVANCE PREPARATION

If any of the clams are open within 4 hours before cooking, cover them with cold water for 5 minutes, then discard any that have not closed. Scrub the clams vigorously, and then refrigerate until ready to cook. Set aside the cooking oil and water.

In a small container, combine the Hot Wok Seasonings; set aside. Soak the mushrooms in hot water until soft, then drain and chop coarsely. In a small bowl, combine all Hot Wok Salsa ingredients; set aside.

HOT WOK ACTION

Place a wok over the highest heat. Add the water. Once it comes to a vigorous boil, add the clams and cover the wok tightly. Steam the clams until they open, about 3 minutes, then slide them into a colander. Discard any clams that have not opened.

Return the wok to the highest heat. Stir-fry the seasonings in the oil, and as soon as they turn white, about 5 seconds, add the Hot Wok Salsa. Bring the salsa to a boil, and then return the clams to the wok. Stir them gently until they are completely glazed with the sauce. Taste and adjust the seasonings. Immediately transfer the stir-fry to a heated platter or dinner plates and serve.

*C*hefs in Asian restaurants stir-fry lobster by chopping live ones into small pieces and tossing them into a hot wok, adding a splash of sauce, and then covering the wok so that the lobster steams until the pieces turn bright red. During the final moments of cooking, the addition of a cornstarch slurry causes the sauce to glaze the lobster pieces. For home preparation, give the lobsters a preliminary steaming (just until they turn red); then slip the barely cooked meat out of the shell, cut it into thin slices, and add the lobster meat to the stir-fry vegetables during the final seconds of cooking.

Thai Lobster with Mint, Ginger, Lime, and Chiles

SERVES 4 AS THE MAIN ENTRÉE

HOT WOK INGREDIENTS

2 2-pound live lobsters

3 baby bok choy

2 whole green onions

½ cup mint leaves, torn into pieces

2 tablespoons cooking oil

HOT WOK SEASONINGS

4 cloves garlic, finely minced

1 tablespoon very finely minced fresh
   ginger

3 fresh serrano chiles, including seeds,
   finely minced

HOT WOK SAUCE

¼ cup orange juice, freshly squeezed

2 tablespoons rice wine or dry sherry

2 tablespoons fish sauce

2 teaspoons finely minced lime zest

1 tablespoon brown sugar

1 tablespoon white wine vinegar

1 tablespoon cornstarch

ADVANCE PREPARATION

Set the lobster aside, and refrigerate. Cut each bok choy stalk on a sharp diagonal, turning over the stalk each time before making another diagonal cut. Cut enough bok choy to fill 4 cups. Cut the green onions on a sharp diagonal into 1-inch lengths. Combine the bok choy and green onions, and refrigerate. In separate containers, set aside the mint leaves and the cooking oil.

In a small bowl, combine the Hot Wok Seasonings; set aside. In another small bowl, combine the Hot Wok Sauce ingredients. Stir well and refrigerate.

HOT WOK ACTION

In a large stockpot, bring 2 inches of water to a vigorous boil over high heat. Add the lobster, head down, cover the pot, and steam for 6 minutes. Then remove the lobster and allow it to cool to room temperature, about 15 minutes. Now twist off the tail, and using the prongs of a fork, pull the tail meat out of the shell. Cut across the meat in ¼-inch-wide slices. Crack the claws and remove the meat, leaving the claw meat whole.

Place a wok over the highest heat. When the wok becomes very hot, add the cooking oil to the center. Roll the oil around the wok and when the oil gives off just a wisp of smoke, add the Hot Wok Seasonings. Stir-fry the seasonings, and as soon as they turn white, about 5 seconds, add the vegetables. Stir and toss the vegetables until the bok choy brightens in color, about 2 minutes.

Stir the Hot Wok Sauce, and then pour it into the wok. Add the lobster meat and mint. Stir and toss until all the ingredients are glazed with the sauce. Taste and adjust the seasonings. Immediately transfer the stir-fry to a heated platter or dinner plates and serve.

*T*hinly sliced pieces of beef tenderloin, chicken breast, or firm fish that are seared in a hot wok make a sensational addition to any salad. This recipe is an example of how the wok can be employed to offer a new twist on a dish from another cuisine. Slices of tuna, marinated in Asian seasonings, are seared in the wok and then crown a Caesar salad. For an equally nice variation, toss the hot stir-fried meat or seafood with the salad greens so that the tuna is evenly glazed with the dressing, and the salad has a pleasant, wilted texture.

Wok-Seared Tuna Caesar

SERVES 4 AS THE MAIN ENTRÉE

HOT WOK INGREDIENTS

1 pound fresh tuna

2 tablespoons thin soy sauce

1 tablespoon dark sesame oil

1 teaspoon Asian chile sauce

1 tablespoon very finely minced fresh ginger

12 cups torn romaine lettuce hearts

1 red bell pepper

3 ounces enoki mushrooms

8 ears fresh baby sweet corn (optional)

1 cup raw cashews

1 cup cooking oil

¾ cup grated imported Parmesan cheese

½ cup cilantro

salt and freshly ground black pepper, to taste

CAESAR SALAD DRESSING

⅓ cup lemon juice, freshly squeezed

1 tablespoon brown sugar

1 tablespoon thin soy sauce

1 tablespoon mayonnaise

½ cup extra virgin olive oil

½ teaspoon Asian chile sauce

½ teaspoon salt

2 cloves garlic

ADVANCE PREPARATION

Cut the tuna into ¼-inch-thick slices. Cut the slices into pieces about 1 inch long and ½ inch wide. In a small bowl, combine soy, sesame oil, chile sauce, and ginger, and then mix thoroughly with the tuna. Marinate the tuna at least 15 minutes but not longer than 8 hours, refrigerated.

Wash and tear romaine leaves. Discard stem and seeds from bell pepper, then chop. Cut off and discard mushroom stems. Pull the mushroom threads apart into individual pieces. Remove the corn husks. In separate containers, set aside and refrigerate the lettuce, bell pepper, mushrooms, and corn.

In a small saucepan, combine the cashews and cooking oil. Place the saucepan over medium heat. Stir the cashews slowly, and when they turn light golden, immediately transfer them to a strainer placed over a heat-proof container. Set aside the nuts and store at room temperature. Reserve 2 tablespoons of the cooking oil.

Set aside the Parmesan. Chop the cilantro. Set aside the salt and pepper. Place all the salad dressing ingredients in an electric blender and blend until completely smooth; transfer the dressing to a small bowl and refrigerate.

HOT WOK ACTION

Combine the lettuce, bell pepper, mushrooms, corn, and cashews in a salad bowl.

Place a wok over the highest heat. When the wok becomes very hot, add the reserved 2 tablespoons of cooking oil to the center. Roll the oil around the wok and when the oil gives off just a wisp of smoke, add the tuna. Stir and toss the tuna just until it loses its raw exterior color.

Immediately transfer the tuna onto the salad greens. Drizzle the salad dressing over the tuna and greens, and toss the salad to evenly combine all the ingredients. Sprinkle on the cilantro, Parmesan, salt, and pepper and toss the salad again. Taste and adjust seasonings, especially for salt. Immediately transfer the salad stir-fry to a platter or dinner plates and serve.

Sizzling Meat Stir-Fries

Wok cooking will revolutionize the way you think about cooking meat. Meat cooked in a wok is ready in seconds, is more tender, and has more intriguing levels of flavor than meat cooked any other way. Searing marinated pieces of meat against the sides of a hot wok traps the moisture inside the meat. The direct high heat causes the marinade's essences to concentrate, cooks the meat in seconds without toughening it, and contributes an earthy low-note flavor to the exterior. Rubbed with Asian seasonings, or spices and herbs from other cuisines, wok-seared meat has applications far beyond the typical Chinese meat-with-vegetable stir-fry. Slide slices of blazing hot chicken out of the wok and onto a simple dinner salad, or toss the chicken with lettuce greens to create a wilted salad that would be admired by any restaurant chef. Stir-fry paper-thin slices of beef tenderloin, marinated in hoisin sauce, rice wine, and chiles, and then wrap the beef, along with spoonfuls of homemade chopped salsa, in hot flour tortillas. Or, sandwich slivers of marinated lamb, just removed from a hot wok, along with slices of vine-ripened tomatoes, lettuce, and coarsely mashed avocado between toasted sesame seed buns. Let these recipes be your guide to wok cooking.

Key Hot Wok Techniques with Meat

■ Choose any raw meat that will be tender with only brief cooking. This means the breast and leg meat from poultry, and the tenderloin and loin from pork, beef, lamb, and veal. Unless you have a special wok burner to properly sear the meat, never stir-fry more than 1 pound of meat.

■ Marinating meat is a key technique. Choose from the meat marinades in this chapter or follow these principles. Limit the amount of marinade to 3 table-spoons for 1 pound of meat. Greater amounts will cause the meat to steam rather than be seared. Including at least 2 teaspoons of oil allows the meat to quickly separate into individual pieces when added to the wok, and prevents the meat from stick-ing to the sides of the wok. Adding 1 teaspoon of cornstarch helps bind the marinade to the meat, and decreases the chance the meat will steam. Marinate the meat at least 15 minutes so that the marinade permeates the meat, but no longer than 2 hours or the meat may become mushy. Some of our favorite marinade ingredients include: chile sauces, citrus zest, dark sesame oil, garlic, ginger, heavy soy sauce, hoisin sauce, honey, oyster sauce, plum sauce, rice wine or dry sherry, serrano chiles, and shallots from around the world.

The next time you decide to crown a dinner salad with meat or seafood blazing hot out of the wok, use the same principal ingredients in both the salad dressing and the marinade. Here the classic Thai flavor combination of fish sauce, honey, chiles, and garlic serves as the marinade and the foundation for an oil-and-vinegar salad dressing.

Thai Chicken Stir-Fry with Baby Lettuce Greens

SERVES 4 AS THE MAIN ENTRÉE SALAD OR 6 TO 10 AS A FIRST COURSE

HOT WOK INGREDIENTS

4 chicken breast halves (about ⅔ pound), boned and skinned

2 tablespoons rice wine or dry sherry

1 tablespoon hoisin sauce

1 tablespoon fish sauce

1 tablespoon honey

1 tablespoon Thai Sriracha chile sauce

3 cloves garlic, finely minced

2 tablespoons very finely minced fresh ginger

8 cups baby lettuce greens or torn lettuce leaves

2 ounces rice sticks

2 cups cooking oil

SALAD DRESSING

3 tablespoons lime juice, freshly squeezed

2 tablespoons fish sauce

2 tablespoons safflower oil

1 tablespoon honey

½ teaspoon Thai Sriracha chile sauce

2 tablespoons slivered basil leaves

1 clove garlic, finely minced

ADVANCE PREPARATION

Cut the chicken crosswise on a sharp bias into ⅛-inch-thick slices. In a small bowl, combine rice wine, hoisin sauce, fish sauce, honey, chile sauce, garlic, and ginger. Mix thoroughly with the chicken slices. Marinate at least 15 minutes but not longer than 8 hours, refrigerated.

Wash, pat dry, and, if necessary, tear the lettuce greens, then refrigerate. Separate the rice sticks into about 10 small bundles. Place the cooking oil in a 10-inch skillet and place over medium-high heat. Heat the oil until a strand of rice stick puffs immediately when added to the oil. Add the rice sticks, about 10 at a time, and when they expand, within 3 seconds, use tongs to turn them over and cook for another 3 seconds. Immediately remove the rice sticks from the oil and drain on paper towels. Continue to cook remaining rice sticks in small amounts. Store the rice sticks in a paper bag at room temperature. Reserve 2 tablespoons of the cooking oil.

In a small bowl, combine the salad dressing ingredients; set aside.

HOT WOK ACTION

Place a wok over the highest heat. When the wok is very hot, add the 2 tablespoons of cooking oil to the center. Roll the oil around the sides of the wok and when the oil just begins to give off a wisp of smoke, add the chicken. Stir and toss until the chicken loses its raw exterior color and is cooked through, about 1 to 2 minutes. Immediately slide the stir-fry onto a platter.

Place the lettuce in a large mixing bowl. Stir the salad dressing, then add the dressing to the lettuce greens and toss to combine evenly. Gently stir in the rice sticks. Place the salad on dinner plates and top with the stir-fried chicken. Serve at once.

Although the Chinese invented the wok, it's not illegal to adapt it to other cooking styles. This Southwest-inspired stir-fry combines stir-fried chicken marinated in a tequila-ginger-chile mixture, topped with crumbled goat cheese, and served with a vine-ripened tomato-cilantro salsa. Try serving the stir-fry with hot corn or flour tortillas and sliced avocados.

Chicken Salsa Explosion

SERVES 4 AS THE MAIN ENTRÉE

HOT WOK INGREDIENTS

4 chicken breast halves (about 1 pound), boned and skinned

1 tablespoon thin soy sauce

1 tablespoon tequila or vodka

1 tablespoon dark sesame oil

3 cloves garlic, finely minced

2 tablespoons very finely minced fresh ginger

3 fresh serrano chiles, including seeds, finely minced

3 ounces soft goat cheese

2 tablespoons cooking oil

HOT WOK SALSA

6 dried Chinese mushrooms

1½ pounds vine-ripened tomatoes

2 ears tender white corn

½ cup chopped green onion

½ cup chopped cilantro

3 tablespoons red wine vinegar

2 tablespoons dark sesame oil

1 tablespoon safflower oil

2 teaspoons cornstarch

1½ teaspoons sugar

½ teaspoon salt

ADVANCE PREPARATION

Cut the chicken breasts lengthwise into 1-inch-wide strips. Then cut across the strips on a sharp bias, making ⅛-inch-wide pieces. In a small bowl, combine the soy sauce, tequila, sesame oil, garlic, ginger, and chiles. Mix thoroughly with the chicken and marinate at least 15 minutes but not longer than 8 hours, refrigerated. Crumble the goat cheese and refrigerate. Set aside the cooking oil.

To prepare the Hot Wok Salsa, cover the dried mushrooms with very hot water and soak until they soften, about 30 minutes. Gently press the water from the mushrooms, discard the stems, and chop. Seed and chop the tomatoes. Cut the kernels off the corn. In a bowl, combine mushrooms, tomatoes, corn, and the remaining salsa ingredients. Mix well and set aside (do not refrigerate).

HOT WOK ACTION

Place a wok over the highest heat. When the wok is very hot, add cooking oil to the center. Roll the oil around the sides of the wok and when the oil just begins to give off a wisp of smoke, add the chicken. Stir and toss until the chicken loses its raw exterior color, about 2 minutes. Stir in the salsa and bring to a rapid boil. Taste and adjust the seasonings. Immediately transfer the chicken to a heated platter or dinner plates. Sprinkle the crumbled goat cheese over the chicken and serve.

oconut milk is made from the hard white interior layer that has been shredded, soaked in hot water, and then pressed to yield coconut milk. A small amount of coconut milk, with its high fat content and subtle flavor, adds a pleasing thickness and richness to stir-fry sauces. Although in this recipe coconut milk is matched with rice wine, oyster sauce, curry, and fresh herbs, coconut milk makes a great addition to many stir-fry dishes. By substituting an equal amount of coconut milk for the chicken stock, orange juice, or rice wine used in any of the Hot Wok Sauces, you will find that the stir-fry sauce acquires a more complex flavor and texture. (Note: Although the rich-tasting chicken thigh meat marries well with coconut milk, chicken breast meat may be used instead.)

Coconut Curry Chicken

SERVES 4 AS THE MAIN ENTRÉE

HOT WOK INGREDIENTS

1 pound chicken thigh meat, boned and
   skinned
1 tablespoon heavy soy sauce
2 tablespoons rice wine or dry sherry
3 tablespoons plus 1 teaspoon cooking oil
1 teaspoon cornstarch
1 small bok choy
3 small Japanese eggplants
4 whole green onions

HOT WOK SEASONINGS

3 cloves garlic, finely minced
2 tablespoons very finely minced fresh
   ginger

HOT WOK SAUCE

½ cup coconut milk
¼ cup rice wine or dry sherry
2 tablespoons oyster sauce
2 teaspoons curry paste or 1 tablespoon
   curry powder
2 teaspoons cornstarch
¼ cup chopped cilantro or basil leaves

ADVANCE PREPARATION

Trim off and discard all fat from the chicken thigh meat. Cut the meat into paper-thin pieces, about ⅛ inch thick. Then cut each piece into ½-inch lengths. In a small bowl, combine the soy sauce, rice wine, 1 teaspoon of the oil, and cornstarch. Mix thoroughly with the chicken slices. Marinate chicken at least 15 minutes but not longer than 8 hours, refrigerated.

Separate the bok choy stems, then cut the stems and leaves on a diagonal into 1-inch lengths. Cut the eggplant in half lengthwise, then place the eggplant together and cut the eggplant crosswise in ¼-inch-thick pieces. Cut the green onions on a sharp diagonal into 1-inch-long pieces. Combine the vegetables together and refrigerate. Divide the cooking oil, putting 2 tablespoons in one container and 1 tablespoon in another; set aside.

In a small container, combine the Hot Wok Seasonings; set aside. In a small bowl, combine the Hot Wok Sauce ingredients, and set aside.

HOT WOK ACTION

Place a wok over the highest heat. When the wok becomes very hot, add 2 tablespoons of cooking oil to the center. Roll the oil around the wok and when the oil gives off just a wisp of smoke, add the chicken. Stir and toss the chicken until it loses its raw exterior color, about 2 minutes, then slide the chicken onto a plate.

Immediately return the wok to the highest heat. Add the remaining 1 tablespoon cooking oil and the Hot Wok Seasonings. Stir-fry the seasonings, and as soon as they turn white, about 5 seconds, add the vegetables. Stir and toss the vegetables until the bok choy turns bright green, about 1 minute, and the eggplant soften (adding a splash of sherry or water and covering the wok for 1 minute will help speed the cooking of the eggplant).

Stir the Hot Wok Sauce, and then pour it into the wok. Stir and toss the vegetables until the eggplant becomes tender, about 1 minute.

Return the chicken to the wok. Stir and toss until all the ingredients are glazed with the sauce. Taste and adjust the seasonings. Immediately transfer the stir-fry to a heated platter or dinner plates and serve.

The magical flavors of tangerine, garlic, oyster sauce, and chiles are a perfect accent used as a barbecue sauce, or as a salad dressing with the addition of a lightly flavored olive oil, or worked into ground beef sirloin to create the world's best hamburger, or combined, as in the following recipe, as a stir-fry sauce. Since citrus juice deteriorates drastically even when refrigerated, squeeze the tangerines or oranges within a few hours of cooking the dish.

Spicy Tangerine Chicken

SERVES 4 AS THE MAIN ENTRÉE

HOT WOK INGREDIENTS

4 chicken breast halves (about 1
  pound), boned and skinned
1 tablespoon heavy soy sauce
1 tablespoon rice wine or dry sherry
1 tablespoon oyster sauce
2 teaspoons minced tangerine or
  orange zest
2 red bell peppers
1 medium zucchini
1 large yellow onion
3 tablespoons cooking oil

HOT WOK SEASONING

4 cloves garlic, finely minced

HOT WOK SAUCE

⅓ cup tangerine or orange juice, freshly
  squeezed
¼ cup rice wine or dry sherry
1 tablespoon oyster sauce
1 tablespoon dark sesame oil
2 teaspoons Asian chile sauce
1 tablespoon cornstarch

ADVANCE PREPARATION

Cut the chicken into ¼-inch-long strips. Cut into ¼-inch cubes. Combine in a small bowl the soy sauce, 1 tablespoon of the rice wine, 1 tablespoon of the oyster sauce, and zest. Mix thoroughly with the chicken. Marinate the chicken at least 15 minutes but not longer than 8 hours, refrigerated.

Seed and stem the peppers, and then cut into ½-inch cubes. Cut the zucchini lengthwise into 4 strips. Place the strips together and cut crosswise into ½-inch pieces. Peel the onion, and cut the onion into thin wedges; then cut each wedge in half. Combine vegetables in a bowl and refrigerate. Divide the cooking oil, putting 2 tablespoons in one container and 1 tablespoon in another; set aside.

Place the garlic in a small container and set aside. In a small bowl, combine the Hot Wok Sauce ingredients and set aside.

HOT WOK ACTION

Place a wok over the highest heat. When the wok becomes very hot, add 2 tablespoons of the cooking oil to the center. Roll the oil around the wok and when the oil just begins to give off a wisp of smoke, add the chicken. Stir and toss the chicken just until it loses its raw exterior color, about 2 minutes, and then slide the chicken onto a plate.

Immediately return the wok to the highest heat. Add the remaining 1 tablespoon of cooking oil and the garlic. When the garlic turns white, about 5 seconds, add the vegetables. Stir and toss the vegetables until they brighten in color, about 2 minutes.

Stir the Hot Wok Sauce, and then add it to the wok. Return the chicken and stir-fry until the sauce thickens enough to glaze the chicken and vegetables. Taste and adjust the seasonings. Immediately transfer the stir-fry to a heated platter or dinner plates and serve.

Stir-fried chicken livers make fantastic appetizers. Be sure to purchase fresh ones that are dark brown and firm. Trim away all the fat and cut any large livers in half. For a variation, stir-fry any of the Hot Wok Seasoning combinations, add the livers to the wok and stir-fry just until they become firm, but are still quite pink in the center. If you want a sauce, add your favorite Hot Wok Sauce during the final minute of cooking.

Chicken Livers with Garlic, Cilantro, and Pine Nuts

SERVES 6 TO 10 AS AN APPETIZER OR 4 AS THE MAIN ENTRÉE

HOT WOK INGREDIENTS

1 pound fresh chicken livers

1 tablespoon finely minced fresh ginger

4 cloves garlic, finely minced

2 tablespoons oyster sauce

1 tablespoon dark sesame oil

1 tablespoon red wine vinegar

1 teaspoon Asian chile sauce

1 teaspoon sugar

¼ cup raw pine nuts

2 vine-ripened tomatoes

2 tablespoons cooking oil

⅓ cup chopped cilantro

ADVANCE PREPARATION

Preheat the oven to 325°. Trim away and discard all fat from the chicken livers. Cut large chicken livers into bite-sized pieces. Set livers aside in the refrigerator.

In a small bowl, combine the ginger, garlic, oyster sauce, sesame oil, red wine vinegar, chile sauce, and sugar; set aside. Toast the pine nuts in the preheated oven until they become light golden, about 8 minutes, then set aside. Thinly slice the tomatoes and arrange them around the edge of a serving platter or dinner plates. In a small container, set aside the cooking oil. In another small container, set aside the cilantro.

HOT WOK ACTION

Place a wok over the highest heat. When the wok becomes very hot, add the cooking oil to the center. Roll the oil around the sides of the wok and when the oil just begins to give off a wisp of smoke, add the livers. Stir and toss until the livers just lose their raw exterior color. Immediately stir in the ginger-sesame oil mixture. Stir and toss the livers until they begin to feel firm, but are still red in the center. Stir in the cilantro and pine nuts. Taste and adjust the seasonings. Immediately transfer the chicken livers to the center of the platter or to dinner plates decorated with tomato slices and serve.

Cleavers

Ting, the legendary Chinese cook, was careful to let his senses and the natural form of ingredients guide his cleaver. In *Changtse*, the fourth-century B.C. Chinese classic, he offered an observation as timeless as his technique:

"A good cook changes his chopper once a year—because he cuts. An ordinary cook once a month—because he hacks. But I have had this chopper for nineteen years, and…its edge is as if fresh from the whetstone."

Behold the Chinese slicing cleaver: its razor-sharp, 8-ounce, rectangular blade slides easily through meats, seafood, and vegetables, and minces green onions and flavor-intense aromatic seasonings in seconds just the way the legendary Ting worked. Using a cleaver has many advantages compared with all other knives. To use a cleaver, visualize Ting and his rhythmic cutting technique. Grasp the handle gently with three fingers while the thumb and index finger rest on either side of the blade to stabilize the cleaver. Never grasp the cleaver by just the handle, or extend the index finger out along the top flat edge of the blade similar to the way one might when cutting with a dinner knife. To minimize the cutting effort, cut with the middle and back half of the cleaver rather than the front edge. Move the cleaver in a circular motion. Direct the cleaver away from your body and down through the food in one easy relaxed motion, and then lift the cleaver slightly upward and return it to its original cutting position. As the cleaver moves in a circular motion, guard the fingers holding the food by slightly extending the knuckles beyond the fingertips that hold the food. Gently press the blade against the knuckles as you cut, while the fingers holding the food inch backward and reveal more food for the blade to cut. To transfer ingredients from the cutting board to a container, slide the blade under the food. As long as the sharp edge of the cleaver angles downward as it slides under the food, there is no chance of cutting the hand that corrals the ingredients.

The quality of cleavers range from heavy European and Chinese meat cleavers that are impossibly awkward to light Chinese slicing cleavers. The latter are designed only to slice, chop, and mince meat, seafood, and vegetables and never for chopping through bones or for other heavy tasks that quickly destroy the blade's razor edge. You will need either a triangular shaped chef's knife or a Chinese slicing cleaver to prepare the recipes in *Hot Wok*. Buy a lightweight Chinese slicing cleaver with a blade that measures approximately 3x8 inches and weighs no more than 10 ounces. The Martin Yan cleaver, which weighs 7 ounces and is sold at cookware shops across the country, and the 10-ounce Dexter stainless cleaver, available at most Asian markets, are top choices.

*M*ost of us associate duck with horribly splattered ovens, smoke-alarm sirens, carving nightmares, and greasy skin everywhere. But if you buy boneless duck breasts, which are easy to skin, or ask your butcher to defrost a whole duck and then bone and skin it for you, the duck meat tastes wonderful stir-fried. Just cut the duck meat into thin, bite-sized pieces and substitute it for an equal amount of the meat in any of these recipes in this book. You will avoid the traditional duck misfortunes, and your guests will marvel at the exotic entrée.

Thai Duck with Cilantro, Chiles, and Garlic

SERVES 4 AS THE MAIN ENTRÉE

HOT WOK INGREDIENTS

1 pound duck breast meat (or meat from 1 whole duck), trimmed of all fat

2 tablespoons hoisin sauce

1 tablespoon rice wine or dry sherry

2 teaspoons cooking oil

3 cups baby string beans

4 whole green onions

1½ cups bean sprouts, perfectly white

3 tablespoons cooking oil

HOT WOK SEASONINGS

5 cloves garlic, finely minced

4 fresh serrano chiles, including seeds, finely minced

HOT WOK SAUCE

⅓ cup chicken stock

¼ cup rice wine or dry sherry

¼ cup chopped cilantro

2 tablespoons fish sauce

1 tablespoon hoisin sauce

1 tablespoon cornstarch

ADVANCE PREPARATION

Cut the duck on a sharp bias into ¼-inch-thick slices. Cut the slices into 1-inch lengths. In a small bowl, combine the hoisin sauce, rice wine, and oil. Mix thoroughly with the duck. Marinate the duck at least 15 minutes but not longer than 8 hours, refrigerated.

Cut off and discard the stem end from the string beans. If the string beans are not very small and tender, place them in a single layer on a dinner plate, cover with plastic wrap, and microwave on high for 1 minute at a time, until they brighten in color. Or, stir the string beans into 2 quarts of boiling water. As soon as they brighten, about 1 minute, immediately transfer to a bowl filled with cold water and ice. When the string beans are thoroughly chilled, remove them from the ice water and pat dry. Cut large string beans into 2-inch lengths. Cut the green onions on a sharp diagonal into 2-inch lengths. Combine the string beans and green onions, and refrigerate. Set aside the bean sprouts. Divide the cooking oil, placing 2 tablespoons in one small container and 1 tablespoon in another; set aside.

In a small bowl, combine the Hot Wok Seasonings; set aside. In another small bowl, combine the Hot Wok Sauce ingredients and set aside, refrigerated.

HOT WOK ACTION

Place a wok over the highest heat. When the wok becomes very hot, add 2 tablespoons of the cooking oil to the center. Roll the oil around the wok and when the oil gives off just a wisp of smoke, add the duck. Stir and toss the duck until it loses its raw exterior color, about 2 minutes, and then slide it onto a plate.

Immediately return the wok to the highest heat. Add the remaining 1 tablespoon of cooking oil, and the Hot Wok Seasonings. Stir-fry the seasonings, and as soon as they turn white, about 5 seconds, add the string beans and green onions. Stir and toss the vegetables until the green onions brighten in color, about 1 minute. Stir the Hot Wok Sauce, and then pour it into the wok.

Return the duck to the wok and add the bean sprouts. Stir and toss until all the ingredients are glazed with the sauce. Taste and adjust the seasonings. Immediately transfer the stir-fry to a heated platter or dinner plates and serve.

Some of the most exciting aspects about stir-frying are the number of variations, improvisations, and cultural culinary borrowings that inspire the imaginations of contemporary wok masters. Here, tender slices of veal and mushrooms are tossed in the wok until barely cooked, and then a wine-cream sauce infused with oyster sauce, garlic, and lemon zest is splashed around the ingredients where it quickly thickens into a beautiful glaze. Accompany this dish with wild rice, rice pilaf, or grilled polenta.

Blackened Veal Scallopini with Fresh Shiitake Mushrooms

SERVES 4 AS THE MAIN ENTRÉE

HOT WOK INGREDIENTS

¼ pound fresh shiitake mushrooms

1 bunch chives

4 tablespoons extra light olive oil

1 pound veal scallopini or cutlets

2 teaspoons crushed Szechwan pepper

1 tablespoon thin soy sauce

2 tablespoons rice wine or dry sherry

2 teaspoons dark sesame oil

HOT WOK SEASONINGS

3 cloves garlic, finely minced

2 small shallots, minced

HOT WOK SAUCE

⅓ cup whipping cream

⅓ cup white wine

1 tablespoon oyster sauce

2 teaspoons dark sesame oil

2 teaspoons finely minced lemon zest

½ teaspoon Asian chile sauce

ADVANCE PREPARATION

Cut off and discard the mushroom stems. Cut the mushrooms into ¼-inch-wide strips. Cut chives into 1-inch lengths. Divide the olive oil, putting 3 tablespoons in one container and 1 tablespoon in another; set aside. Cut the veal into rectangles about ½-inch wide and 1 inch long. Within 30 minutes of cooking, rub the veal with Szechwan pepper, soy sauce, rice wine, and sesame oil.

In a small container, combine Hot Wok Seasonings and set aside. In another small bowl, combine Hot Wok Sauce ingredients and set aside.

HOT WOK ACTION

Place a wok over the highest heat. When the wok becomes very hot, add 3 tablespoons of the olive oil to the center. Roll the oil around the wok, and when the oil gives off just a wisp of smoke, add the Hot Wok Seasonings. Stir-fry the seasonings, and as soon as they turn white, about 5 seconds, add the mushrooms. Stir and toss the mushrooms for a few seconds, and then add the Hot Wok Sauce. Bring to a rapid boil, and cook until the mushrooms soften and the sauce thickens enough to lightly coat a spoon, about 2 minutes. Immediately slide the mushrooms and sauce into a bowl.

Quickly wipe out the wok with paper towels, and then return the wok to the burner over highest heat. When the wok becomes very hot, about 1 minute, add the remaining 1 table-spoon of olive oil to the center. Roll the oil around the wok, and when the oil gives off just a wisp of smoke, add the veal. Stir and toss the veal until it loses its raw outside color, about 2 minutes.

Immediately return the mushrooms and the sauce to the wok. Add the chives, and stir all the ingredients until evenly mixed. Taste and adjust the seasonings. Immediately transfer the stir-fry to a heated platter or dinner plates and serve.

Searing marinated, thinly sliced pork in a hot wok instantly seals in the moisture and produces meat that is incredibly tender. Use pork tenderloin, rather than pork loin, for all stir-fry dishes. The tenderloin is virtually fat free, easy to cut against the grain, and one large tenderloin weighs enough for a stir-fry dish to serve as the main entrée for two to four.

Thai Pork with Mint and Chiles

SERVES 4 AS THE MAIN ENTRÉE

HOT WOK INGREDIENTS

1 pound pork tenderloin

1 tablespoon rice wine or dry sherry

1 tablespoon fish sauce

1 tablespoon honey

4 small dried red chiles

1 red onion

2 vine-ripened tomatoes

4 cups sugar snap peas

3 tablespoons cooking oil

1½ cup peanuts, toasted

HOT WOK SEASONING

3 cloves garlic, finely minced

HOT WOK SAUCE

2 teaspoons minced orange zest

⅓ cup orange juice, freshly squeezed

3 tablespoons rice wine or dry sherry

2 tablespoons fish sauce

1 tablespoon honey

1 tablespoon cornstarch

⅓ cup slivered mint leaves

ADVANCE PREPARATION

Trim all fat from sides of pork. Cut across the pork tenderloin in ⅛-inch-thick slices. Overlap the slices and cut into 1-inch rectangular pieces. In a small bowl, combine the rice wine, fish sauce, and honey. Then mix thoroughly with the pork and marinate at least 15 minutes but not longer than 8 hours, refrigerated.

Remove and discard seeds from dried chiles. Leave chiles in large pieces. Peel the onion, cut into 8 wedges, and cut each wedge in half. Cut the tomatoes in half through the middle, squeeze out their seeds, and then cut them into thin wedges. Combine the chiles and vegetables, then set aside. Divide the oil, putting 2 tablespoons in one small container and 1 tablespoon in another. Toast peanuts as described on page 17.

In a small container, set aside the garlic. In a small bowl, combine the Hot Wok Sauce ingredients and refrigerate.

HOT WOK ACTION

Place a wok over the highest heat. When the wok becomes very hot, add 2 tablespoons of the cooking oil to the center. Roll the oil around the wok and when the oil gives off just a wisp of smoke, add the pork. Stir and toss the pork until it loses its raw exterior color, about 2 minutes, and then slide the pork onto a plate.

Immediately return the wok to the highest heat. Add the remaining 1 tablespoon of cooking oil, and the garlic. Stir-fry, and as soon as the garlic turns white, about 5 seconds, add the vegetables. Stir and toss the vegetables until the onion separates, about 1 minute. Stir the Hot Wok Sauce, and then pour it into the wok.

Return the pork to the wok. Add the peanuts. Stir and toss until all the ingredients are glazed with the sauce. Taste and adjust the seasonings. Immediately transfer the stir-fry to a heated platter or dinner plates and serve.

N ot one of our friends can resist warm Chinese or Mexican flour wrappers brushed with rich-tasting hoisin sauce and filled with shredded pork, mushrooms, cabbage, and green onions. The contrasting textures and sublime taste always elicit chants of "mu shu, mu shu" as guests assemble more. Mu shu wrappers are available frozen at all Asian markets, or substitute the thinnest flour tortillas.

Classic Mu Shu Pork

SERVES 8 AS AN APPETIZER OR 4 AS THE MAIN ENTRÉE

HOT WOK INGREDIENTS

1 tablespoon heavy soy sauce

1 tablespoon rice wine or dry sherry

4 teaspoons dark sesame oil

1 pound pork tenderloin, cut into ¼-inch matchstick pieces

½ pound fresh mushrooms, thinly sliced

2 cups slivered green cabbage

1 red bell pepper, slivered

4 whole green onions, slivered

12 mu shu wrappers or flour tortillas

½ cup hoisin sauce

4 eggs

¼ cup cooking oil

HOT WOK SEASONINGS

2 cloves garlic, finely minced

1 tablespoon very finely minced fresh ginger

HOT WOK SAUCE

3 tablespoons chicken stock

2 tablespoons rice wine or dry sherry

2 teaspoons heavy soy sauce

2 teaspoons dark sesame oil

2 teaspoons cornstarch

½ teaspoon sugar

¼ teaspoon freshly ground black pepper

¼ teaspoon salt

ADVANCE PREPARATION

In a bowl, combine the soy sauce, rice wine, and 2 teaspoons of sesame oil. Mix thoroughly with the pork and marinate at least 15 minutes but not longer than 8 hours, refrigerated.

Combine the mushrooms, cabbage, bell pepper, and green onions and refrigerate. Wrap mu shu pancakes in aluminum foil if heating in an oven or in plastic wrap if heating in the microwave, sealing well to form an airtight package; set aside. Set aside hoisin sauce. Combine eggs with remaining 2 teaspoons of sesame oil, then beat until well mixed. Divide the cooking oil, placing 2 tablespoons in one container and 1 tablespoon each in two containers; set aside.

In a small container, combine the Hot Wok Seasonings; set aside. In a small bowl, combine the Hot Wok Sauce ingredients and set aside.

HOT WOK ACTION

Preheat an oven to 325°. Place the foil package of mu shu wrappers in the preheated oven and warm for 10 minutes, or heat in a microwave.

Meanwhile, place a wok over the highest heat. When the wok becomes very hot, add 2 tablespoons of the cooking oil to the center. Roll the oil around the wok and when the oil gives off just a wisp of smoke, add the pork. Stir and toss the pork until it loses its raw exterior color, about 2 minutes, and then slide the pork onto a plate.

Immediately return the wok to the highest heat. Add 1 tablespoon cooking oil, and roll the oil around the sides of the wok. Add the eggs. Scramble the eggs until they're no longer runny, them slide then onto the plate of pork.

Immediately return the wok to the highest heat. Add the remaining 1 tablespoon cooking oil, and the Hot Wok Seasonings. Stir-fry the seasonings, and as soon as they turn white, about 5 seconds, add the vegetables. Stir and toss the vegetables until the green onion and cabbage brighten in color, about 1 minute. Stir the Hot Wok Sauce and then pour it into the wok. Add the pork and scrambled eggs.

Stir and toss until all the ingredients are glazed with the sauce. Taste and adjust the seasonings. Immediately transfer the stir-fry to a heated platter or dinner plates and serve with hoisin sauce and warm mu shu wrappers. To assemble, each person spoons a little hoisin sauce on a wrapper, adds some of the filling, and rolls up the wrapper.

No cooking technique other than stir-frying allows such a startling range of variations, additions, substitutions, omissions, and outright culinary creativity. Once the simple rules of cutting, marinating, and the basic elements of stir-frying are understood, stir-frying becomes an improvisational cooking technique that is ideally suited for today's fast-paced lifestyle. If you review the section on the basic stir-fry rules (Hot Fire, Hot Wok, Hot Action), and follow this simple outline, you will be able to create a different stir-fry dish every day based on your own food preferences and the availability of ingredients.

Hot Creations: How to Improvise Your Own Wok Dishes

Meat Selection

Choose any raw meat that will be tender with only brief cooking. Cut ¼ to 1 pound of meat into very small pieces no larger than ½-inch cubes, 1 x ½ x ¼-inch rectangles, or 1 x ¼-inch matchstick pieces. Marinate at least 15 minutes but no longer than 2 hours in any of the meat marinades from the second chapter, Sizzling Meat Stir-Fries.

Seafood Selection

Choose ¼ to 1 pound of raw shrimp, scallops, squid, or firm-fleshed fish such as tuna, shark, or swordfish. Shell, devein, and butterfly the shrimp, or split the shrimp in half lengthwise. If using large scallops, thinly slice. Clean squid as described on page 26. Cut fish into 1 x ½ x ¼-inch rectangles.

Vegetable Selection

Prepare enough non-leafy vegetables to equal 4 to 5 cups. Review how to cut and prepare the vegetables for stir-frying, which is explained on page 61.

Hot Wok Seasoning and Hot Wok Sauce Selections

Choose any Hot Wok Seasoning and mince finely. Choose any Hot Wok Sauce and combine the ingredients.

The Classic Stir-Fry Order

When you want to duplicate the look of classic Chinese stir-fry dishes that integrate meat or seafood with vegetables, follow this outline. Cut the meat or seafood and the vegetables into small sizes suitable for stir-frying. Prepare a Hot Wok Seasoning and a Hot Wok Sauce. Here are the Hot Wok Action steps:

1. Heat the wok over highest heat until very hot. Add 1 tablespoon of cooking oil to the center of the wok, and roll the oil around the sides.

2. When the oil just begins to give off a wisp of smoke, add the **meat** or **seafood**. Stir-fry until the color changes, about 1 minute, and then immediately slide the **meat** or **seafood** onto a plate.

3. Return the wok to the highest heat, and add 1 tablespoon of cooking oil. Immediately add the **Hot Wok Seasonings** and stir-fry for 10 seconds.

4. Immediately add the **vegetables**. Stir-fry the **vegetables** until they brighten in color, about 2 minutes.

5. Immediately add the **Hot Wok Sauce**. Return the **meat** or **seafood** to the wok. Continue stir-frying until the sauce glazes all the ingredients and thickens slightly, about 1 minute.

6. Transfer the stir-fry to a heated platter or dinner plates and serve at once.

Variations on the Classic Stir-Fry Order

For meat or seafood stir-fries without any vegetables, begin with step 1, then add the **Hot Wok Seasonings**, and the **meat** or **seafood**. When the **meat** or **seafood** changes color, add the **Hot Wok Sauce** and stir-fry until the sauce glazes the food.

For vegetarian stir-fry dishes, eliminate step 2. Once the oil becomes hot, add the **Hot Wok Seasonings** for step 3 and proceed with steps 4, 5 and 6.

For stir-fries with meat or seafood positioned on top of stir-fried vegetables, stir-fry the **vegetables** first and then place these on a heated platter or on dinner plates. Then stir-fry the **Hot Wok Seasonings**, add the **meat** or **seafood**, and when the color changes, add the **Hot Wok Sauce**. When the sauce glazes the food, position the **meat** or **seafood** in the center of the stir-fried **vegetables**.

For stir-frying previously cooked meat or seafood, follow the directions above for vegetarian stir-fry dishes. At the very end of the stir-fry process, add up to ½ pound cold cooked **meat** or **seafood** (barbecued chicken, chilled shrimp, broiled salmon) and stir-fry with the **vegetables** and **Hot Wok Sauce** until the **meat** or **seafood** is reheated.

nexpensive beef flank steak, flap meat, and tri-tip have much more flavor than beef tenderloin. Using a razor-sharp knife, slice these economy cuts across the grain into paper-thin slices so the meat will not be tough when stir-fried. Or, to guarantee perfect results every time without tedious cutting, purchase beef tenderloin. Regardless of whether the meat is cut with or against the grain, in thin or thick slices, beef tenderloin seared in a hot wok is always tender.

Beef Tenderloin with Wild Mushrooms

SERVES 4 AS THE MAIN ENTRÉE

HOT WOK INGREDIENTS

1 pound beef tenderloin, fat trimmed

1 tablespoon heavy soy sauce

1/4 cup plus 1 tablespoon rice wine or dry sherry

2 teaspoons dark sesame oil

1 pound mixed fresh mushrooms (chanterelles, shiitakes, portabellos, morels, and buttons)

3 whole green onions

3 tablespoons cooking oil

HOT WOK SEASONINGS

3 cloves garlic, finely minced

1 tablespoon very finely minced fresh ginger

HOT WOK SAUCE

1/4 cup chicken stock

2 tablespoons rice wine or dry sherry

1 tablespoon thin soy sauce

1 tablespoon oyster sauce

1 tablespoon dark sesame oil

1 tablespoon cornstarch

1/2 teaspoon sugar

1/4 teaspoon freshly ground black pepper

ADVANCE PREPARATION

Cut the beef in 1/4-inch-thick slices. Cut each slice into rectangular pieces, about 1/2 inch wide and 1 inch long. In a small bowl, combine the soy sauce, 1 tablespoon of rice wine, and sesame oil. Then mix thoroughly with the beef and marinate at least 15 minutes but not longer than 8 hours, refrigerated. Set aside the remaining 1/4 cup rice wine.

Trim tough stems from mushrooms. Cut the mushrooms into 1/4-inch-thick slices. Cut the green onions on a sharp diagonal into 1-inch-long pieces and then combine with the mushrooms. Divide the cooking oil, putting 2 tablespoons in one small container and 1 tablespoon in another, and set aside.

In a small bowl, combine the Hot Wok Seasonings; set aside. In another small bowl, combine the Hot Wok Sauce ingredients and set aside.

HOT WOK ACTION

Place a wok over the highest heat. When the wok becomes very hot, add 2 tablespoons of the cooking oil to the center. Roll the oil around the wok and when the oil gives off just a wisp of smoke, add the beef. Stir and toss the beef until it loses its raw exterior color, about 2 minutes, and then slide the beef onto a plate.

Immediately return the wok to the highest heat. Add the remaining 1 tablespoon of cooking oil, and the Hot Wok Seasonings. Stir-fry the seasonings, and as soon as they turn white, about 5 seconds, add the mushrooms and green onions. Stir and toss the mushrooms until the green onions brighten in color and the mushrooms soften slightly, about 3 minutes. As you stir-fry the mushrooms, add the remaining 1/4 cup rice wine, so that the mushrooms soften more quickly and develop a fuller flavor.

Stir the Hot Wok Sauce, and then pour it into the wok. Return the beef to the wok. Stir and toss until all the ingredients are glazed with the sauce. Taste and adjust the seasonings. Immediately transfer the stir-fry to a heated platter or dinner plates and serve.

For this stir-fry dish, a Thai red curry sauce glazes shreds of beef tenderloin, green bell pepper, and onion. Each person spreads extra red curry sauce on warm flour tortillas, adds a portion of the stir-fry along with slices of avocado, and folds the tortilla into a soft taco or rolls it into a burrito. Break the routine of always serving stir-fry dishes as entrées by presenting this dish as an appetizer using smaller tortillas, or try this cold as a picnic dish. It's fantastic!

Beef Fajitas with Smoking Thai Red Curry Sauce

SERVES 4 AS THE MAIN ENTRÉE

HOT WOK INGREDIENTS

1 pound beef tenderloin, fat trimmed, cut into ¼-inch matchstick pieces

1 red onion

1 green pepper, cut into 1-inch lengths, ¼-inch-wide

1 small wedge of jicama, cut into ¼-inch-wide slices

8 8-inch flour tortillas

1 large ripe avocado

½ lemon or lime

3 tablespoons cooking oil

SMOKING THAI RED CURRY SAUCE

¼ cup chipotle chiles in adobo sauce, puréed

2 vine-ripened tomatoes, seeded and chopped

2 shallots, chopped

4 cloves garlic, chopped

1 tablespoon chopped fresh ginger

¼ cup red wine vinegar

2 tablespoons brown sugar

2 tablespoons fish sauce

1 teaspoon ground cumin seeds

1 teaspoon cornstarch

ADVANCE PREPARATION

In a small bowl, set aside the beef. Peel the onion, cut off and discard its bottom and top, and then cut it into ¼-inch-wide wedges. Combine the onion, pepper, and jicama and refrigerate. Stack the tortillas and wrap tightly with aluminum foil, or in plastic wrap if heating them in the microwave; set aside. Split the avocado in half. Remove the seed and scoop out the flesh. Unless avocado is cut less than 10 minutes in advance of serving the dish, squeeze a little lemon juice over the avocado slices. Divide the oil, putting 2 tablespoons in one small container and 1 tablespoon in another.

Combine all Thai Red Curry Sauce ingredients and blend in an electric blender until completely smooth. Add ¼ cup Thai Red Curry Sauce to the beef and mix thoroughly, then refrigerate at least 15 minutes but not longer than 8 hours. In a small bowl, set aside ¼ cup Thai Red Curry Sauce to use as the stir-fry sauce. In a small saucepan, set aside remaining sauce for brushing across the tortillas.

HOT WOK ACTION

Preheat the oven to 325°. Place tortillas in the preheated oven for 10 minutes or heat them in the microwave. Bring the sauce to a low boil, simmer for 5 minutes; transfer to a decorative bowl and set aside.

Place a wok over the highest heat. When the wok becomes very hot, add 2 tablespoons of the cooking oil to the center. Roll the oil around the wok. When the oil just begins to give off a wisp of smoke, add the beef. Stir and toss the beef until it just loses its raw exterior color, about 2 minutes, and then slide it onto a plate.

Immediately return the wok to the highest heat. Add the remaining 1 tablespoon of cooking oil, and roll the oil around the side of the wok. When the oil just begins to give off a wisp of smoke, add the vegetables. Stir and toss until the onion separates into individual segments and softens slightly.

Immediately return the beef to the wok. Add ¼ cup Smoking Thai Red Curry Sauce. Stir and toss to combine evenly. Taste and adjust seasonings. Transfer the stir-fry to a heated platter or heated dinner plates. Serve with a bowl of the Smoking Thai Red Curry Sauce, avocado slices, and hot flour tortillas. To assemble, each person spreads a little of the sauce on a tortilla, adds the stir-fried mixture, and an avocado slice, and rolls up the tortilla.

Ground beef, lamb, or lean pork, marinated and seared in a hot wok, makes a quick, inexpensive, and delicious stir-fry dish. Try substituting ground meat in any of this book's meat stir-fry dishes. Simply work the marinade into the meat with your fingers so that every grain of meat becomes moistened. When you cook the meat in the hot wok, press the meat vigorously with the back of a spoon to break it apart into small pieces. After the preliminary stir-frying of ground meat, always transfer to a colander to drain excess oil.

New Age Chili

SERVES 4 AS THE MAIN ENTRÉE

HOT WOK INGREDIENTS

¼ cup plus 2 tablespoons rice wine or
 dry sherry

1 tablespoon heavy soy sauce

1 tablespoon oyster sauce

1 pound ground beef

1 large Vidalia onion

½ pound button mushrooms

2 cups shelled fresh peas

3 tablespoons cooking oil

HOT WOK SEASONINGS

5 cloves garlic, finely minced

1 tablespoon very finely minced fresh
 ginger

HOT WOK SAUCE

½ cup rice wine or dry sherry

2 tablespoons oyster sauce

1 tablespoon hoisin sauce

1 tablespoon dark sesame oil

1 tablespoon cornstarch

2 teaspoons curry powder

1 teaspoon Asian chile sauce

ADVANCE PREPARATION

In a medium-sized bowl, combine 2 tablespoons of rice wine, 1 tablespoon of soy sauce, and 1 tablespoon oyster sauce. Add the beef and work in the marinade with your fingers; refrigerate. Set aside the remaining rice wine.

Cut off and discard the ends from the onion. Cut the onion into thin wedges, and then cut each wedge into cubes. Cut each mushroom into quarters. In a bowl, combine the onion, mushrooms, and peas and refrigerate. Divide the cooking oil in half and set aside.

In a small container, combine the Hot Wok Seasonings; set aside. In a small bowl, combine the Hot Wok Sauce ingredients and set aside.

HOT WOK ACTION

Place a wok over the highest heat. When the wok becomes very hot, add half the cooking oil to the center. Roll the oil around the wok and when the oil gives off just a wisp of smoke, add the beef. Stir and toss the beef, pressing it against the sides of the wok, until it breaks into individual pieces and loses its raw color, about 2 minutes. Slide the beef into a colander.

Immediately return the wok to the highest heat. Add the remaining cooking oil and the Hot Wok Seasonings. Stir-fry the seasonings, and as soon as they turn white, about 5 seconds, add the vegetables. Stir and toss the vegetables until the onion separates and the peas brighten in color, about 2 minutes. As you stir-fry add the remaining ¼ cup rice wine, so that the mushrooms soften and develop a fuller flavor.

Stir the Hot Wok Sauce, and then pour it into the wok. Return the beef to the wok. Stir and toss until all the ingredients are glazed with the sauce. Taste and adjust the seasonings. Immediately transfer the stir-fry to a heated platter or dinner plates and serve.

Though rarely found on Chinese menus in this country, lamb is eaten by millions of Chinese Muslims in northern and western China. When trimmed of all the exterior fat, the rich taste of lamb makes it a perfect partner for scallions, leeks, onions, and peppers, as well as for the assertive seasonings of garlic, ginger, chiles, hoisin, bean sauce, and dark sesame oil. Lamb is delicious substituted for the meat in any Chinese, Thai, or Vietnamese stir-fry dish. When buying lamb, purchase the upper end of the leg rather than the shank. To reduce the preparation time, ask the butcher to remove the bone and trim off all fat.

Mongolian Lamb with Shredded Scallions

SERVES 4 AS THE MAIN ENTRÉE

HOT WOK INGREDIENTS

1 pound meat from leg of lamb, fat trimmed

1 tablespoon hoisin sauce

1 tablespoon heavy soy sauce

1 tablespoon rice wine or dry sherry

2 teaspoons dark sesame oil

4 cloves garlic, finely minced

4 whole green onions

2 cups fresh bean sprouts

2 tablespoons cooking oil

HOT WOK SAUCE

1 tablespoon rice wine or dry sherry

1 tablespoon heavy soy sauce

1 tablespoon dark sesame oil

2 teaspoons red wine vinegar

1 teaspoon Asian chile sauce

1 teaspoon cornstarch

¼ teaspoon sugar

¼ teaspoon salt

ADVANCE PREPARATION

Cut the lamb into ⅛-inch-thick slices. Overlap the slices and cut into matchstick pieces, about ¼ inch wide. In a small bowl, combine the hoisin sauce, 1 tablespoon of soy sauce, rice wine, sesame oil, and garlic. Mix thoroughly with the lamb and marinate the lamb at least 15 minutes but not longer than 8 hours, refrigerated.

Cut the green onions lengthwise into very thin slivers. Then cut the slivers into 1½-inch lengths, and refrigerate. Set aside the bean sprouts. In a small container, set aside the cooking oil. In a small bowl, combine the Hot Wok Sauce ingredients and set aside.

HOT WOK ACTION

Place a wok over the highest heat. When the wok becomes very hot, add the cooking oil to the center. Roll the oil around the wok, and when the oil gives off just a wisp of smoke, add the lamb. Stir and toss the lamb until it loses its raw exterior color, about 2 minutes.

Immediately stir in the green onions. Stir and toss the green onions to evenly combine. Stir the Hot Wok Sauce, and then pour it into the wok. Stir and toss until all the ingredients are glazed with the sauce. Taste and adjust the seasonings. Stir in the bean sprouts, and immediately transfer the stir-fry to a heated platter or dinner plates and serve.

Anytime dinner guests are involved in simple preparation activities, such as folding dumplings, sprinkling toppings on pizza dough, or, in this case, filling hot corn or flour tortillas with a spicy stir-fry lamb dish, the informal atmosphere generates more animated conversation.

Spicy Thai Lamb Tacos

HOT WOK INGREDIENTS

1 pound meat from leg of lamb, fat trimmed

2 yellow onions

4 vine-ripened plum tomatoes

12 6-inch corn tortillas or 8 8-inch flour tortillas

2 tablespoons cooking oil

1 cup cilantro sprigs or mint leaves

2 ripe avocados

HOT WOK MARINADE/SAUCE

2 tablespoons hoisin sauce

2 tablespoons rice wine or dry sherry

1 tablespoon plum sauce

1 tablespoon honey

1 tablespoon Thai Sriracha chile sauce

1 teaspoon cornstarch

4 cloves garlic, finely minced

2 tablespoons very finely minced fresh ginger

1 tablespoon minced lemon zest

ADVANCE PREPARATION

Cut the meat into strips about ½ inch wide. Cut across the strips in ⅛-inch-thick slices.

Cut off and discard the ends from the onions. Cut the onions into very thin wedges. Cut the tomatoes in half, squeeze out the seeds, and cut them into thin wedges. In a small bowl, combine the onions and tomatoes and refrigerate. Stack the tortillas and wrap tightly with aluminum foil if heating in the oven, or wrap tightly in plastic wrap if heating in the microwave. Divide the cooking oil in half and set aside in small containers. Set aside the cilantro sprigs.

Split the avocados in half. Remove the seeds and scoop out the flesh. Cut the avocados into ¼-inch-wide slices. (If prepared more than 10 minutes before serving the dish, sprinkle the slices with a little lemon or lime juice.)

In a bowl, combine all the ingredients for the Hot Wok Marinade and stir well. Add ¼ cup Hot Wok Marinade/Sauce to the meat and mix thoroughly. Marinate the lamb at least 15 minutes but no longer than 8 hours, refrigerated. Set aside remaining marinade/sauce to use as the Hot Wok Sauce.

HOT WOK ACTION

Preheat the oven to 325°. Place the tortillas in the preheated oven for 10 minutes or warm in the microwave.

Place a wok over the highest heat. When the wok becomes very hot, add 1 tablespoon of cooking oil to the center. Roll the oil around the wok. When the oil just begins to give off a wisp of smoke, add the lamb. Stir and toss the lamb until it loses its raw exterior color, about 2 minutes, and then slide the lamb onto a plate.

Immediately return the wok to the highest heat. Add the remaining 1 tablespoon of cooking oil and add the vegetables when the oil becomes hot. Stir and toss until the onion separates into individual segments and the tomatoes soften.

Add the marinade/sauce. Return the lamb to the wok. Stir and toss until all the ingredients are glazed with the sauce. Taste and adjust the seasonings. To assemble, each person spoons a little of the stir-fry onto a tortilla, adds avocado slices, seasons the filling with cilantro, and then rolls up the tortillas.

For a quick supper after a hard day at work, add previously cooked meats, such as meat from stews, curries, and barbecues to vegetables stir-fried in the wok. In the following recipe, lamb shanks simmer until tender in a rich cinnamon, garlic, soy sauce, and wine mixture. Then the meat is cut into bite-sized pieces, and stir-fried hours later with garden vegetables. If the left-over meat has any sauce or gravy, add ¼ to ½ cup of this at the end of the stir-fry process to unify the flavors of the dish.

Garlic Lamb Shanks with Crisp Garden Vegetables

SERVES 4 AS THE MAIN ENTRÉE

SOY BRAISING LIQUID

½ cup heavy soy sauce

1 cup red wine

¼ cup brown sugar

1 tablespoon orange zest

Juice from 3 oranges

2 cinnamon sticks

2 teaspoons whole cloves

4 cloves garlic, crushed

5 small dried whole red chiles

4 cups water

HOT WOK INGREDIENTS

4 lamb shanks

1 small bok choy

2 whole green onions, slivered

2 cups slivered purple cabbage

½ pound button mushrooms, thinly sliced

2 tablespoons cooking oil

HOT WOK SEASONINGS

6 cloves garlic, finely minced

1 tablespoon very finely minced fresh
   ginger

HOT WOK SAUCE

2 tablespoons rice wine or dry sherry

1 tablespoon cornstarch

ADVANCE PREPARATION

In a saucepan just large enough to hold the shanks snugly, combine the Soy Braising Liquid. Bring to a low boil, cover, and simmer for 1 hour. Then add lamb shanks to the liquid and simmer until they become tender, about 2½ hours. Remove shanks, and cut the meat into bite-sized pieces. If done more than an hour before stir-frying, return meat to the liquid and refrigerate. Reserve ⅓ cup of the braising liquid.

Separate the bok choy stems, then cut the stems and leaves on a diagonal into 1-inch lengths. In a container, combine bok choy, green onions, cabbage, and mushrooms, and refrigerate. In a small container, set aside the cooking oil.

In a small container, combine the Hot Wok Seasonings; set aside. In a small bowl, combine the Hot Wok Sauce ingredients and add ⅓ cup of the Soy Braising Liquid. Stir well, and refrigerate.

HOT WOK ACTION

If the lamb shank meat has been soaking in the soy sauce liquid, remove the lamb with a slotted spoon. Place a wok over the highest heat. When the wok becomes very hot, add the cooking oil to the center. Roll the oil around the wok and when the oil gives off just a wisp of smoke, add the Hot Wok Seasonings. Stir-fry a few seconds, and then add the vegetables. Stir and toss the vegetables until the bok choy turns bright green, about 1 minute.

Add the lamb shanks to the wok. Stir the Hot Wok Sauce, and then pour it into the wok. Stir and toss until all the ingredients are glazed with the sauce. Taste and adjust the seasonings. Immediately transfer the stir-fry to a heated platter or dinner plates and serve.

Chopsticks

"Two slim sticks are made in a round shape and blunted, the length of a man's hand and as thick as a quill for writing. They can pick up anything, no matter how tiny it is, very cleanly and without soiling their hands. For that reason they do not use table-cloths or napkins or even knives, as everything comes to the table minutely cut up. When they want to eat it, they bring the bowl in close to their mouth and then, with those two sticks, are able to fill their mouth with marvelous agility and swiftness."

—Francesco Carletti, seventeenth-century Jesuit missionary

Woks, cleavers, and chopsticks form the kitchen triumvirate that gives Chinese cooking its defining characteristics. While they may not be essential for today's high-tech kitchens, each has many unique characteristics that greatly enhance the cuisine's offerings. Forks, for example, seem like crude implements compared with chopsticks. Forks conduct heat, have a metallic taste, and can damage the texture of food. Chopsticks, especially those made from bamboo, conduct no heat, have a neutral taste, and require everyone from novice cooks to hot wok masters to constantly decide which morsel to savor next.

The name "chopsticks" comes from the pidgin English "chop, chop," meaning "quick, quick" and indeed the Chinese liken the action of chopsticks to that of "quick little boys." To use, the bottom chopstick stays stationary while the top one moves. Beyond this basic principle, there is no orthodox grip. Avoid crossing the chopsticks at the tips, or allowing the tips to become uneven. The quickest way to master chopsticks is to rely on them not only for eating *Hot Wok* food, but also for many kitchen tasks, such as beating eggs, mixing batter, and tasting sauces.

From Garden to Hot Wok

Woks and vegetables, in their few minutes of culinary courtship, achieve a perfect gastronomic marriage. The searing heat seals the moisture (and thus the vitamins and minerals) within the vegetables, intensifies their natural sweetness by caramelizing the sugars, fully cooks vegetables in seconds while retaining their distinctive natural textures, adds a subtle undercurrent of satisfying low-note flavors, and transforms the colors into brilliant hues. Wok cook baby snow peas, adding as a final accent a splash of rice wine and dark sesame oil. Stir and toss a selection of mushrooms, such as shiitakes, portabellos, and chanterelles, with a drizzle of oyster sauce and dry sherry. Sear pencil-thin asparagus and slivered red bell pepper with minced garlic until their colors intensify and then finish the dish with only sea salt and freshly ground black pepper. Whether served as an important accompaniment to the main entrée, or as the centerpiece of an elegant vegetarian meal, stir-fry vegetables always play a starring role.

Key Hot Wok Techniques with Vegetables

- The vegetables used in this book's recipes are only suggested selections; you may substitute any other vegetables that require similar cooking times. Just choose the freshest vegetables, cut no more than 4 to 5 cups of vegetables into the same size pieces, and then follow The Classic Stir-Fry Cooking Order steps 4, 5, and 6 (page 50).

- Short-cooking vegetables include the following: **thin asparagus**, **baby green beans**, **Chinese long beans**, **cabbages** (white cabbage, red cabbage, Napa cabbage, bok choy), **celery**, **Japanese eggplant** cut into ¼-inch-thick slices, **mushrooms** (buttons, shiitakes, portabellos, chanterelles, honeys, and morels but not oysters or enokis, because they become mushy when stir-fried), **onions** (yellow, red, and white onions, green onions, and chives), **peas** (garden peas, snow peas, sugar snap peas), **peppers** and **chiles** (all the various colored sweet peppers, as well as the entire range of spicier peppers and chiles), **summer squash** (zucchini, crookneck, patty pan and all other squashes that become tender with brief cooking), and fresh **water chestnuts.** You may use any combination of the above, as long as you use a total of 5 cups or less.

■ Long-cooking vegetables, which require longer cooking because of their dense textures, include: **thick asparagus**, **broccoli**, **brussels sprouts**, **carrots**, **cauliflower**, **potatoes**, **string beans**, and **yams**. To accelerate the cooking process in meat and seafood stir-fry dishes, cut the vegetables into small pieces, and then briefly microwave them, or blanch them in boiling water just until they brighten, and then chill the vegetables in ice water. At this point, they can be combined with short-cooking vegetables, again, as long as the total amount of vegetables does not exceed 5 cups. On the other hand, in vegetable stir-fry dishes, add the long-cooking raw vegetables to the wok, stir-fry these a few seconds, and then add about ½ cup liquid (water, wine, sherry, water that dried mushrooms were softened in, or chicken stock), cover the wok, and steam-cook the vegetables just until they brighten. Then add any short-cooking vegetables, stir-fry until they brighten, add a Hot Wok Sauce, and serve at once.

■ Up to 2 cups of leafy greens, including all kinds of lettuces and bean sprouts and spinach, can be added to any type of stir-fry dish at the very end of the stir-fry process.

The fruity, mildly sour taste of tamarind juice makes it an ideal addition when stir-frying chicken, shrimp, and vegetables such as zucchini, Chinese long beans, bok choy, and baby carrots. Tamarind pods, which grow on large trees throughout the tropics, contain a reddish brown pulp that is processed into black 8-ounce and 1-pound bricks, wrapped in clear plastic, and sold at room temperature in all Asian, Mexican, and Latin America markets. To use, break off a thumb-sized piece of the pulp and place it in a bowl with just enough hot water to cover. After it has soaked 10 to 15 minutes, rub the softened pulp between your fingers and then strain the juice through a sieve and discard the pulp.

Baby Carrots in Tamarind Glaze

SERVES 4 AS A SIDE DISH

HOT WOK INGREDIENTS

3 bunches baby carrots (about ¾ pound)

6 fresh water chestnuts (optional)

1 tablespoon chopped chives

2 tablespoons white sesame seeds

2 tablespoons cooking oil

¼ cup water

HOT WOK SEASONINGS

2 cloves garlic, finely minced

1 tablespoon very finely minced fresh ginger

HOT WOK SAUCE

⅓ cup tamarind juice

¼ cup rice wine or dry sherry

2 tablespoons honey

2 teaspoons cornstarch

¼ teaspoon Asian chile sauce

ADVANCE PREPARATION

Trim and discard the carrot ends. Cut enough carrots in half on a sharp diagonal to fill 4 cups. Peel the water chestnuts. Set aside the chives. Place sesame seeds in an ungreased sauté pan, place over medium heat, and stir until they turn light golden. Immediately transfer the sesame seeds to a small dish. In separate small containers, set aside the cooking oil and water.

Combine the Hot Wok Seasonings in a small container and set aside. In a small bowl, combine the Hot Wok Sauce ingredients, then refrigerate.

HOT WOK ACTION

Place a wok over the highest heat. When the wok becomes very hot, add the cooking oil to the center. Roll the oil around the wok and when the oil begins to give off just a wisp of smoke, add the Hot Wok Seasonings.

Stir-fry the seasonings, and as soon as they turn white, about 5 seconds, add the carrots and water chestnuts. Stir and toss the carrots for a few seconds and then add the water. Immediately cover the wok and steam the carrots until they brighten in color, about 2 minutes.

Stir the Hot Wok Sauce, and then pour it into the wok. Stir and toss until the carrots are glazed with the sauce. Taste and adjust the seasonings. Immediately transfer the carrots to a heated platter or dinner plates. Sprinkle on the chives and toasted sesame seeds and serve at once.

Salted black beans, chiles, and peppers are as classic a combination in Chinese cooking as garlic, basil, and olive oil are in Italian cuisine. The sweet, fruity, high notes of peppers are further heightened by the spicy contribution of a small quantity of minced fresh serrano chiles. Adding a dramatic backdrop, the salted, fermented black beans make the peppers and chiles taste sweeter and cause all the flavors to linger on the palate.

Sizzling Bell Peppers with Black Beans and Chiles

SERVES 4 AS A SIDE DISH

HOT WOK INGREDIENTS

1 red bell pepper

1 green bell pepper

1 yellow bell pepper

1 orange bell pepper

1 yellow onion

2 tablespoons cooking oil

¼ cup cilantro sprigs or slivered mint leaves

HOT WOK SEASONINGS

3 cloves garlic, finely minced

2 fresh serrano chiles, including seeds, finely minced

HOT WOK SAUCE

3 teaspoons rice wine or dry sherry

1½ tablespoons dark sesame oil

2 teaspoons hoisin sauce

1 teaspoon oyster sauce

1 teaspoon black bean sauce

2 teaspoons cornstarch

ADVANCE PREPARATION

Discard the stems and seeds from the bell peppers. Cut the peppers into ½-inch-wide strips. Place the strips together and cut the strips into 1½-inch lengths. Cut off and discard the top and bottom of the onion. Cut the onion into narrow wedges. Place all the vegetables together and refrigerate. In separate small containers, set aside the cooking oil and cilantro or mint.

Set aside the Hot Wok Seasonings in a small container. In a small bowl, combine Hot Wok Sauce ingredients and set aside.

HOT WOK ACTION

Chop the cilantro. Place a wok over the highest heat. When the wok becomes very hot, add the cooking oil to the center. Roll the oil around the wok, and when the oil gives off just a wisp of smoke, add the Hot Wok Seasonings. Stir-fry the seasonings, and as soon as they turn white, about 5 seconds, add the vegetables. Stir-fry the vegetables until they brighten in color, about 3 to 4 minutes.

Stir the Hot Wok Sauce, and then pour it into the wok. Stir and toss until the vegetables are glazed with the sauce, about 1 minute. Stir in the cilantro or mint. Taste and adjust the seasonings. Immediately transfer the vegetables to a heated platter or dinner plates and serve.

L eafy greens offer a challenge to stir-fry artists. Think of stir-fried leafy greens as similar to a hot wilted salad. Cooked just seconds too long, the leafy greens wilt into a watery mess, and in the case of spinach, pick up an unpleasant metallic taste from the side of steel woks. For perfectly stir-fried greens, toss the fresh greens in a large bowl with about the same amount of liquid seasonings you would use for a salad. Then stir-fry the greens in a wok for just seconds so that some of the leaves are not even wilted when the dish is transferred from the wok onto a platter.

Seared Spinach

SERVES 4 AS A SIDE DISH

HOT WOK INGREDIENTS

12 cups tender spinach leaves, loosely
    packed
2 tablespoons pine nuts
3 cloves garlic, finely minced
2 tablespoons cooking oil
¼ cup cilantro sprigs
1 tablespoon dark sesame oil
1 tablespoon oyster sauce
1 tablespoon rice wine or dry sherry
1 teaspoon sugar
1 teaspoon Asian chile sauce

ADVANCE PREPARATION

Preheat the oven to 325°. Thoroughly wash and dry the spinach leaves. Discard the stems from the spinach leaves, and then refrigerate the spinach leaves.

Toast the pine nuts in the preheated oven until golden, about 8 minutes. In separate containers, set aside the toasted pine nuts, garlic, cooking oil, and cilantro. In a small bowl, combine the sesame oil, oyster sauce, rice wine, sugar, and chile sauce.

HOT WOK ACTION

In a large bowl, toss the spinach with the sesame oil mixture until all the leaves are evenly coated. Place a wok over the highest heat. When the wok becomes very hot, add the cooking oil to the center. Roll the oil around the wok and when the oil gives off just a wisp of smoke, add the garlic and then the spinach leaves.

Stir and toss the spinach, quickly turning the spinach over so that it wilts evenly. When about three-fourths of the spinach leaves have wilted, about 30 seconds, immediately transfer the spinach to a heated platter or dinner plates. Sprinkle on the pine nuts and cilantro serve at once.

Complex layers of flavor explode with each bite. The tender eggplant, saturated with the rich-tasting sauce, also contributes textural contrasts with the ground lamb and crisp sweet bell pepper. Serve this with plenty of steamed rice, or use the garlicky eggplant, omitting the lamb, as a hot or cold Chinese ratatouille to accompany all types of meat just off the barbecue grill.

Hot Garlic Eggplant with Lamb

SERVES 4 AS A SIDE DISH

HOT WOK INGREDIENTS

4 medium Japanese or Chinese
    eggplant
1 red onion
1 red bell pepper
3 tablespoons cooking oil

HOT WOK SEASONINGS

¼ pound ground lamb
8 cloves garlic, finely minced
2 small shallots, minced
1 tablespoon hoisin sauce

HOT WOK SAUCE

⅓ cup rice wine or dry sherry
2 tablespoons oyster sauce
1 tablespoon hoisin sauce
1 tablespoon red wine vinegar
1 tablespoon Asian chile sauce
1 tablespoon dark sesame oil
2 teaspoons brown sugar
¼ cup chopped cilantro

ADVANCE PREPARATION

Cut off and discard the ends from eggplant. Cut eggplant in half lengthwise, then cut across eggplant to make ½-inch-thick pieces. You should have about 4 cups of eggplant. Peel the onion, then cut into ½-inch cubes. Stem and seed the pepper, then cut into ½-inch pieces. Combine the vegetables in a bowl and refrigerate.

In a small container, set aside the cooking oil. In another small container, combine the Hot Wok Seasonings, mix thoroughly, and refrigerate. In a small bowl, combine the Hot Wok Sauce ingredients and set aside.

HOT WOK ACTION

Place a wok over the highest heat. When the wok becomes very hot, add the cooking oil to the center. Roll the oil around the wok and when the oil gives off just a wisp of smoke, add the Hot Wok Seasonings. Stir-fry the seasonings, pressing the ground lamb against the sides of the wok. Stir and toss the seasonings until the lamb loses all of its pink color and breaks into small fragments, about 2 minutes.

Add the vegetables to the wok. Stir-fry for a few seconds, and then add the Hot Wok Sauce, and immediately cover the wok. Steam the vegetables for 30 seconds, and then temporarily remove the cover, stir the vegetables, and then cover the wok. Continue to steam until the eggplant is soft, about 4 minutes.

When the eggplant becomes soft, remove the top and stir-fry the vegetables until all the sauce disappears, about 1 minute. Taste and adjust the seasonings. Immediately transfer the vegetables to a heated platter or dinner plates and serve.

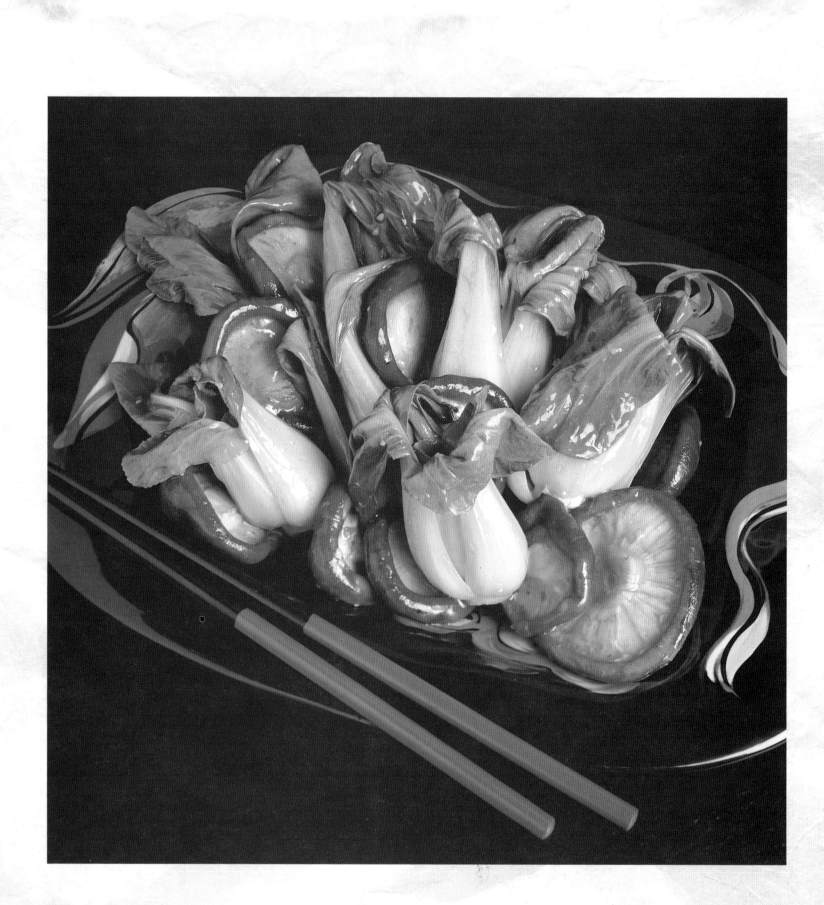

This classic Cantonese dish contrasts the crunchy, mild cabbage flavor of bok choy with the chewy texture and meaty flavor of giant dried Chinese mushrooms. Sold at markets and herbal shops in Chinese communities, these mushrooms must be submerged in water for several hours in order to soften them. When buying dried Chinese mushrooms, look for large ones with thick caps that are criss-crossed with deep crevices. If dried Chinese mushrooms are unavailable, substitute fresh shiitake mushrooms (sold in the produce section of most American supermarkets). Just cut off the stems, and stir-fry the mushrooms with the bok choy until the mushrooms begin to soften.

Baby Bok Choy with Giant Chinese Mushrooms

SERVES 4 AS A SIDE DISH

HOT WOK INGREDIENTS

16 giant dried Chinese mushrooms
8 baby bok choy or 1 large bok choy
2 tablespoons cooking oil

HOT WOK SEASONINGS

3 cloves garlic, finely minced
1 large shallot, finely minced

HOT WOK SAUCE

¼ cup chicken stock
¼ cup rice wine or dry sherry
2 tablespoons oyster sauce
1 tablespoon dark sesame oil
1 tablespoon cornstarch
½ teaspoon sugar
freshly ground black pepper, to taste

ADVANCE PREPARATION

Place the dried mushrooms in a bowl, cover the mushrooms with the hottest tap water, and place a small plate on top of the mushrooms so that the mushrooms are kept submerged. Soak the mushrooms until they soften, about 1 hour. When they become soft, gently squeeze out most of the water. Cut off and discard the tough mushroom stems, then cut the mushrooms in half.

Cut baby bok choy in half lengthwise. If using large bok choy, cut off and discard the bottom end. Separate bok choy stalks. Cut each stalk on a sharp diagonal, and after each cut turn the stalk over and make another sharp diagonal cut to create diamond-shaped pieces. (You will need a total of 4 to 5 cups of vegetables.) Cut the large leaves into 2 or 3 pieces. Combine the vegetables in a bowl and refrigerate. In a small container, set aside the cooking oil.

Combine the Hot Wok Seasonings, and set aside in a small container. In a small bowl, combine the Hot Wok Sauce ingredients and set aside.

HOT WOK ACTION

Place a wok over the highest heat. When the wok becomes very hot add the cooking oil to the center. Roll the oil around the wok, and when the oil gives off just a wisp of smoke, add the Hot Wok Seasonings. Stir-fry the seasonings, and as soon as they turn white, about 5 seconds, add the vegetables.

Stir and toss the vegetables until the bok choy leaves begin to wilt and turn bright green, about 3 minutes. Stir the Hot Wok Sauce, and then pour it into the wok. Stir and toss until the vegetables are glazed with the sauce, about 1 minute. Taste and adjust the seasonings. Immediately transfer the vegetables to a heated platter or dinner plates and serve.

f you cut shallow notches down the length of each zucchini before slicing it crosswise into thin coins, the dish is more attractive, and the notches, which trap the sauce, give the zucchini a more intense flavor. The sweet crunch of the candied walnuts adds a great texture and flavor contrast when sprinkled across any vegetable, shrimp, or chicken stir-fry. The candied nuts can be made months ahead and stored in the freezer.

Zucchini Coins with Garlic and Candied Walnuts

SERVES 4 AS A SIDE DISH

HOT WOK INGREDIENTS

3 yellow zucchini

3 green zucchini

3 whole green onions

½ pound walnut halves

2 tablespoons honey

2 tablespoons sugar

2 tablespoons water

⅛ teaspoon salt

2 tablespoons cooking oil

HOT WOK SEASONING

4 cloves ginger, finely minced

HOT WOK SAUCE

¼ cup rice wine or dry sherry

3 tablespoons tomato sauce

2 tablespoons thin soy sauce

1 tablespoon dark sesame oil

2 teaspoons cornstarch

¼ teaspoon finely ground black pepper

ADVANCE PREPARATION

Cut off and discard the zucchini ends. Using a small knife, cut three long, equally spaced notches down the length of each zucchini. Slice the zucchini into ¼-inch-wide pinwheels (to make about 4 cups). Cut the green onion on a diagonal into 1-inch pieces. Place the vegetables together in a bowl and refrigerate.

To prepare the candied walnuts, preheat the oven to 350°. Line a baking sheet with foil, and spray the foil with nonstick cooking spray. Place the walnuts in a small saucepan. Cover the nuts with hot water, place the saucepan over high heat, and boil the walnuts for 5 minutes. Immediately transfer the walnuts to a colander to drain. In a 2-quart saucepan, add the honey, sugar, water, and the salt. Bring this to a boil over medium heat, then add the walnuts. Stir the nuts until the mixture becomes dry, about 4 minutes. Spread the nuts in an even layer on the baking sheet, and place the baking sheet in the preheated oven. Cook the nuts until they turn a light mahogany color, about 12 minutes. During the roasting, turn the nuts over every 5 minutes. When the nuts become mahogany colored, remove the baking sheet from the oven, and as the nuts cool, break them apart

into individual pieces with your fingers. Store in an airtight container for 1 day at room temperature, or freeze indefinitely.

In a small container, set aside the cooking oil. In another small container, set aside the ginger. In a small bowl, combine the Hot Wok Sauce ingredients and set aside.

HOT WOK ACTION

Place a wok over the highest heat. When the wok becomes very hot, add the cooking oil to the center. Roll the oil around the wok and when the oil gives off just a wisp of smoke, add the ginger. Stir-fry the ginger, and as soon as it turns white, about 5 seconds, add the vegetables.

Stir and toss the vegetables until the zucchini brightens, about 3 minutes. Stir the sauce, and then pour it into the wok. Stir and toss until the vegetables are glazed with the sauce, about 1 minute. Taste and adjust the seasonings. Immediately transfer the vegetables to a heated platter or dinner plates, sprinkle on the candied walnuts, and serve.

This stir-fry dish contains both long- and short-cooking vegetables. Because the cooking times vary, longer-cooking vegetables (in this case, cauliflower) are partially cooked beforehand. This can be completed hours in advance. Later, when you stir-fry the vegetables, all the par-cooked vegetables as well as short-cooking vegetables, such as mushrooms and cabbage, go into the wok at the same time. At the moment the short-cooking vegetables become brightly colored but are still crunchy, the long-cooking vegetables will have reheated and become perfectly cooked.

Thai Rainbow Garden Vegetables

SERVES 4 AS A SIDE DISH

HOT WOK INGREDIENTS

2 cups cauliflower florets

¼ pound snow peas

¼ pound Chinese long beans

2 small vine-ripened tomatoes

¼ pound button mushrooms

¼ small green cabbage

2 tablespoons cooking oil

HOT WOK SEASONINGS

4 cloves garlic, finely minced

1 tablespoon very finely minced fresh ginger

2 fresh serrano chiles, including seeds, finely minced

HOT WOK SAUCE

⅓ cup coconut milk

3 tablespoons rice wine or dry sherry

2 tablespoons oyster sauce

1 tablespoon honey

2 teaspoons curry powder

2 teaspoons cornstarch

1 tablespoon chopped cilantro

1 tablespoon chopped basil leaves

1 tablespoon chopped mint leaves

2 teaspoons finely minced lime zest

ADVANCE PREPARATION

Cut the cauliflower florets into bite-sized pieces. Place the cauliflower in a single layer on a dinner plate, cover with plastic wrap, and microwave on high for 1 minute at a time, until the cauliflower becomes tender. Or, stir the cauliflower into 2 quarts of boiling water. As soon as the cauliflower becomes tender, about 1 minute, immediately transfer it to a bowl filled with cold water and ice. When the cauliflower is thoroughly chilled, drain and pat dry.

Snap off the stem ends from the snow peas and set aside (you should have about 1 cup). Cut off and discard the stem ends from the long beans; then cut the long beans on a diagonal into 1- to 2-inch lengths (yields about 1 cup), and set aside. Cut the tomato in half through the middle, squeeze out the seeds, and cut into thin wedges. Cut the mushrooms into quarters. Shred enough cabbage to yield 1 cup. In a large bowl, combine all the vegetables and refrigerate. Set aside the cooking oil in a small container.

Set aside the Hot Wok Seasonings in a small container. In a small bowl, combine the Hot Wok Sauce ingredients and set aside.

HOT WOK ACTION

Place a wok over the highest heat. When the wok becomes very hot, add the cooking oil to the center. Roll the oil around the wok and when the oil gives off just a wisp of smoke, add the Hot Wok Seasonings. Stir-fry the seasonings, and as soon as they turn white, about 5 seconds, add the vegetables.

Stir and toss the vegetables until the cabbage brightens, about 2 minutes. Stir the Hot Wok Sauce, and then pour it into the wok. Stir and toss until the vegetables are glazed with the sauce, about 1 minute. Taste and adjust the seasonings. Immediately transfer the vegetables to a heated platter or dinner plates and serve.

One of the most famous Szechwan dishes, this is attributed to the inventive old pock-marked wife of Chef Chen Ling-fu, and her wondrous way of stir-frying soft bean curd with mounds of garlic, ground pork, a fistful of chiles, and plenty of green onions or cilantro. The very soft, almost cooling texture of bean curd acts as a perfect foil balanced against the assertive accompanying flavors. To vary the dish dramatically, just substitute the Hot Wok Sauce from Spicy Tangerine Chicken (page 40) or Beef Fajitas with Smoking Thai Red Curry Sauce (page 53). As you stir-fry the bean curd, very gently capsize the bean curd to ensure that the cubes remain whole while the sauce reduces into a glaze. Since bean curd is high in protein (the Chinese call it "meat without bones"), serve Ma Po Do Fu as a main entrée with rice and a salad.

Ma Po Do Fu

SERVES 4 AS A SIDE DISH

HOT WOK INGREDIENTS

1 pound fresh firm bean curd

3 whole green onions, minced

1 cup cilantro sprigs

2 tablespoons cooking oil

HOT WOK SEASONINGS

1/4 pound ground lamb or pork

6 large cloves garlic, finely minced

1 tablespoon very finely minced fresh
    ginger

HOT WOK SAUCE

1/2 cup chicken stock

3 tablespoons rice wine or dry sherry

1 tablespoon thin soy sauce

1 tablespoon oyster sauce

1 tablespoon Asian chile sauce

1 tablespoon dark sesame oil

2 teaspoons cornstarch

1 teaspoon heavy soy sauce

1/4 teaspoon finely ground Szechwan
    pepper

ADVANCE PREPARATION

Cut the bean curd into 1/2-inch cubes, then refrigerate. In a small bowl, set aside the minced green onions. Set aside cilantro sprigs. In a small container, set aside cooking oil.

In a small container, combine the Hot Wok Seasonings and mix thoroughly. In a bowl, combine the Hot Wok Sauce ingredients and refrigerate.

HOT WOK ACTION

Chop the cilantro and set aside. Place a wok over the highest heat. When the wok becomes very hot, add the cooking oil to the center. Roll the oil around the wok and when the oil gives off just a wisp of smoke, add the Hot Wok Seasonings. Stir-fry the seasonings, pressing the ground meat against the sides of the wok. Stir and toss the seasonings until the meat loses all of its pink color and breaks into small fragments, about 2 minutes.

Add the bean curd and green onions to the wok. Gently turn over the bean curd, and then stir the Hot Wok Sauce and add it to the wok. Immediately cover the wok, and steam-cook the bean curd for 30 seconds. Then remove the cover, sprinkle in the chopped cilantro, and gently turn the bean curd over. Continue cooking the bean curd, gently turning it over until the sauce thickens and glazes all the ingredients, about 2 minutes. Taste and adjust the seasonings. Immediately transfer the bean curd to a heated platter or dinner plates and serve.

f you scan this recipe's ingredient list you will not find a reference to lobster or anything evenly remotely associated with the ocean. In classic Cantonese cooking, "lobster sauce" refers to the same black bean sauce used in Lobster Cantonese. Garlicky and slightly nutty (from dark sesame oil), the sauce resonates with the earthy, salty, fermented black beans' flavor, and richness from egg stirred into the sauce at the last minute. The Cantonese are passionate about their black bean sauces, and add the sauce to steamed whole fish, stir-fried clams, wok-seared crabs, and many vegetable dishes.

Asparagus in Lobster Sauce

SERVES 4 AS A SIDE DISH

HOT WOK INGREDIENTS

2 bunches fresh asparagus, medium thickness

½ cup pine nuts

1 tablespoon unsalted butter, room temperature

1 tablespoon cooking oil

1 egg

¼ cup water

HOT WOK SEASONING

2 cloves garlic, finely minced

HOT WOK SAUCE

½ cup chicken stock

2 tablespoons rice wine or dry sherry

1 tablespoon dark sesame oil

2 teaspoons black bean sauce

2 teaspoons cornstarch

1 teaspoon sugar

⅛ teaspoon finely ground white pepper

ADVANCE PREPARATION

Preheat the oven to 325°. Snap off and discard the tough asparagus stems. Cut the asparagus on a sharp diagonal into 2-inch-long pieces, then refrigerate.

Toast the pine nuts in the preheated oven until they turn golden, about 8 minutes. In a small bowl, combine the butter and cooking oil; set aside. In separate containers, set aside the egg, water, and garlic. In a small bowl, combine the Hot Wok Sauce ingredients and refrigerate.

HOT WOK ACTION

Beat egg well. Place a wok over the highest heat. When the wok becomes very hot, add the butter and the cooking oil to the center. Roll the oil and butter around the wok and when the butter begins to bubble, add the garlic.

Stir-fry the garlic, and as soon as it turns white, about 5 seconds, add the asparagus. Stir and toss the asparagus for a few seconds, and then add the water. Immediately cover the wok and steam the asparagus until it turns bright green, about 2 minutes.

Stir the Hot Wok Sauce, and then pour it into the wok. Stir and toss until the asparagus is glazed with the sauce. Remove the wok from the heat, and stir in the egg. Then stir in the pine nuts. Taste and adjust the seasonings. Immediately transfer the asparagus to a heated platter or dinner plates and serve.

When stir-frying mushrooms, always choose fresh mushrooms that have a firm texture such as buttons, chanterelles, morels, porcinis, portabellos, and shiitakes. During the stir-fry process, they maintain their dense texture and acquire a wonderfully complex flavor from the stir-fry sauce. Avoid soft-textured mushrooms such as oysters and enokis, which become flabby.

Mushroom Fantasy Stir-Fry

SERVES 4 AS A SIDE DISH

HOT WOK INGREDIENTS

1½ pounds mixed fresh mushrooms
(shiitakes, chanterelles, portabellos, buttons)
1 large bunch chives
2 tablespoons unsalted butter, room temperature
2 tablespoons cooking oil
¼ cup white wine

HOT WOK SEASONINGS

3 cloves garlic, finely minced
2 large shallots, minced

HOT WOK SAUCE

⅓ cup white wine
1 tablespoon oyster sauce
2 teaspoons cornstarch
1 teaspoon tomato paste
½ teaspoon sugar
¼ teaspoon Asian chile sauce
2 teaspoons fresh thyme leaves

ADVANCE PREPARATION

Discard the tough stems from the mushrooms. Cut the mushrooms into ¼-inch slices, quarters, or wedge-shaped pieces, to fill 4 to 6 cups, and then refrigerate. Chop the chives and refrigerate. In a small container, combine the butter and oil and set aside.

Set aside ¼ cup white wine. Combine the Hot Wok Seasonings and set aside in a small container. In a small bowl, combine the Hot Wok Sauce ingredients.

HOT WOK ACTION

Place a wok over the highest heat. When the wok becomes very hot, add the butter and oil to the center. Roll the butter and oil around the wok and when the butter begins to bubble, add the Hot Wok Seasonings.

Stir-fry the seasonings, and as soon as they turn white, about 5 seconds, add the mushrooms. Stir and toss the mushrooms until they soften slightly, about 3 minutes. As you stir-fry the mushrooms, add the white wine so that the mushrooms soften more quickly and develop a fuller flavor.

Stir the Hot Wok Sauce, and then pour it into the wok. Stir and toss until the mushrooms are glazed with the sauce. Taste and adjust the seasonings. Stir in the chives. Immediately transfer the mushrooms to a heated platter or dinner plates and serve.

The choice of which beverage to serve with *Hot Wok* food should be guided by personal preferences and the dominant flavors in each recipe. Matching a dish with an appropriate beverage creates a magical interaction, as the major flavor components of the food and beverage are accented and understated flavors come to the forefront. Wok dishes that are delicate in flavor with an undertone of sweetness will go best with chilled light-bodied beers, slightly sweet sakes, German Riesling Kabinetts, and California Sauvignon Blancs (Fume Blanc), Chenin Blancs, and Riesling wines. When chiles are a primary ingredient in a dish, dark beers, the sweeter sakes, iced teas, and moderately priced sparkling wines are all good choices. Let this just be a general guide. Follow your own instincts, serve a variety of wines and other drinks, and let the festivities begin.

Hot Wok Drinks

Beer

First introduced in the Far East by nineteenth-century German brewmasters, beer is a wonderful match for the assertive flavors and dramatic taste variations of wok cooking. We have enjoyed drinking beer throughout our travels in the Far East and with these *Hot Wok* recipes. Dishes with a mild combination of flavors, such as Soft-Shell Crab Bonanza (page 24), are perfectly enhanced by many of the lighter Asian beers like Tsing Tao from China, Sapporo from Japan, and Singha from Thailand. But, again, when chiles play the starring role, we prefer a chilled dark beer such as San Miguel from the Philippines or Dos Equis from Mexico, both of whose toasty taste and creamy body stand up to the assertive chile flavor and quickly prepare the palate for the next taste sensation.

Sake

Sake or Japanese-style rice wine has been an important part of Japanese cultural heritage for more than 2,000 years. With an alcohol content of 16 percent, this clear wine has a smooth, mellow flavor, no aftertaste, and ranges from very dry to sweet. Usually associated just with Japanese food, sake goes well with the entire spectrum of Chinese and Thai dishes. Serving small containers of hot sake adds an exotic element to the dinner, sparks conversation, and stimulates the palate for more *Hot Wok* food. Sake ranges from "sweet," with a residual sugar totaling up to 3 percent, to very dry with as little sugar as .03 percent. Sweet-tasting sakes, which are the least expensive, should be served hot and matched with spicy food, such as Spicy Tangerine Chicken (page 40) or Curried Coconut Noodles with Mint and Basil (page 89). To heat sake, if it is in a large bottle, pour a smaller amount into a sake container and place it in barely simmering water. Heat until the wine becomes hot (110°), or microwave on high for one minute at a time until it is hot. The more expensive dry sakes, labeled as "premium sake," have a residual sugar content of 1 percent or less, and should be served chilled with such non-spicy dishes as Classic Mu Shu Pork (page 48).

Tea

Hot Chinese tea is a good match with the entire range of *Hot Wok* food, except for the spicy dishes because the tannins in the tea cause spicy food to taste hotter. The tea plant is a member of the camellia family (*Thea sinensis*). Leaves are picked throughout the year, and graded according to shape and size. Green tea comes from the smallest leaves which, soon after picking, are dried over charcoal. Green tea is a compatible beverage with the mildest dishes. Black tea is made by fermenting the leaves before drying over charcoal, and contains caffeine and tannins. Semi-fermented teas are mixed with scented buds, such as jasmine and lychee flowers, and can add a delicate floral accent to a mild dish. For the spicy *Hot Wok* dishes, nothing is more refreshing than iced Chinese hibiscus "tea" sold in all Asian markets under the brand name Ten Ren Roselle tea. Its lack of tannins and the naturally sweet taste soothe the palate.

Wine

When serving *Hot Wok* dishes, a good choice of wine will enhance the flavors of the food and the wine itself will attain new flavor complexities as the enthusiasm of your dinner guests increases throughout the evening. Moderately priced sparkling wines (California champagne-style wine), particularly *blanc de noir*, go with all the recipes in this book. Non-spicy dishes that use salt-rich flavorings, such as oyster sauce, fish sauce, soy sauce, and black beans, pair best with light white wines, low in alcohol (less than 12 percent), and with good acidity such as those from Alsace, Muscadet, and Sancerre; dry German white wines; and California Sauvignon Blanc (Fume Blanc). Non-spicy, generally sweet *Hot Wok* dishes such as Sizzling Lemon Shrimp on Puff Pastry (page 11), and Baby Carrots in Tamarind Glaze (page 63), should be matched with wines that have some sweetness. Choose German Riesling Kabinetts, California Chenin Blancs, Rieslings, and White Zinfandels with 1 to 3 percent residual sugar. Spicy *Hot Wok* dishes marry best with moderately priced sparkling wines from California, Spain, Italy, and France. The carbonation has a pleasant soothing effect with even the most spicy dishes. In addition, red wines such as Zinfandel, Pinot Noir, and Merlot work well with meat dishes such as Classic Mu Shu Pork (page 48), Blackened Veal Scallopini with Fresh Shiitake Mushrooms (page 45), and dishes such as Thai Duck with Cilantro, Chiles, and Garlic (page 43), when the chiles have been greatly reduced or eliminated so that the balance of the red wine is not destroyed.

CREATE HEALTHY PASTA AND RICE DISHES...

New Hot Wok Triumphs with Pasta and Rice

Wok cooking provides the perfect way to create healthy pasta and rice dishes with visual appeal and flavor-intense characteristics. No other cooking utensil than the wok cradles such a large amount of pasta or rice, provides such a large surface area for very quick cooking, or allows for the vigorous, rhythmic stirring and tossing to evenly integrate pasta and rice with all the other ingredients of a dish. No other cooking technique produces one-dish menus with so little effort and so much flavor. Try stir-frying cooked pasta with one of the Hot Wok Sauces, such as the oyster sauce, tomato sauce, and dark sesame oil trio from Soft-Shell Crab Bonanza (page 24) to create a simple side dish. Another night, stir-fry tiger prawns with asparagus, button mushrooms, left-over cold cooked rice, and the complex-flavored Hot Wok Sauce from page 89 to produce a stunning main entrée for a dinner party. Or, solve a work-night menu dilemma by stir-frying vegetables until brightly colored, and then add pasta along with the previous night's remaining pot roast for an easy dinner. Whatever your choice, the results will be spectacular.

Key Hot Wok Techniques with Pasta & Rice

■ There are a few easy-to-remember rules when planning a stir-fry pasta or rice dish. Choose a dried pasta that takes at least 5 minutes to cook. Shorter cooking dried pastas and all "fresh" pastas have too soft a texture to maintain their shape during the stir-frying process. Precook the pasta and rice. This can be completed up to a day in advance of the last-minute stir-frying. For pasta, boil 1 to 8 ounces in 5 quarts of rapidly boiling water, following the cooking instructions on the package. When the pasta just becomes al dente, immediately drain it in a colander, rinse with cold water, drain thoroughly again, and then toss with up to 2 tablespoons of cooking oil to prevent it from sticking together. For rice, we prefer long-grain white rice rather than any kind of brown rice. Brown rice has such a distinctive taste that it often overwhelms the nuances of the Hot Wok Seasonings and Hot Wok Sauces. To cook white rice, follow the directions on page 97.

■ Follow The Classic Stir-Fry Order steps on page 50. As soon as the vegetables brighten, add the cold cooked pasta or rice. Use any ratio of vegetables and pasta or rice not to exceed a total of 8 cups. (Traditional Chinese pasta and rice dishes have twice as much pasta or rice as vegetables and only a tiny amount of seafood or meat.) Stir and toss 1 minute to start reheating the pasta or rice, and then add the Hot Wok Sauce. Continue stir-frying until the sauce glazes all the ingredients and the pasta or rice is piping hot, about 3 more minutes. Taste and adjust the seasonings and serve at once.

Pity Chinese chefs who, mired in the traditional use of spaghetti and fettuccine noodles for all their pasta dishes, have stubbornly resisted the bold Italian pastas invading contemporary American kitchens. Pastas, such as fusilli, penne, farfalle, tecozette, radiatore, conchigliette, and pastina-orzo, or the latest shape or color perfected by Italian designers, make a wonderful foundation for all stir-fry dishes. It's only a matter of time before bowties, small tubes, rippled shells, and dramatic spirals will be incorporated into Chinese cuisine.

Tricolor Fusilli with Wild Mushrooms

SERVES 6 TO 8 AS A SIDE DISH OR 4 AS THE MAIN ENTRÉE

HOT WOK INGREDIENTS

½ pound mixed fresh mushrooms
(chanterelles, shiitakes, portabellos,
morels, buttons)
1 cup small snow peas
3 whole green onions
½ cup pine nuts
6 ounces dried tricolor fusilli
2 tablespoons cooking oil
2 tablespoons unsalted butter
¼ cup rice wine or dry sherry

HOT WOK SEASONINGS

4 cloves garlic, finely minced
2 large shallots, finely minced

HOT WOK SAUCE

½ cup chicken stock
¼ cup rice wine or dry sherry
2 tablespoons oyster sauce
1 tablespoon dark sesame oil
1 tablespoon cornstarch
2 teaspoons fresh thyme leaves
1 teaspoon tomato paste
1 teaspoon Asian chile sauce

ADVANCE PREPARATION

Preheat an oven to 325°. Trim the tough stems from the mushrooms. Cut the mushrooms into ¼-inch-thick slices, then set aside. Snap the stem end off each snow pea, pulling away the fiber that runs along the top ridge. Cut the green onions on a sharp diagonal into ½-inch lengths. Combine with the snow peas and green onions and refrigerate. Toast the pine nuts in the preheated oven until they turn golden, about 8 to 12 minutes. Set aside the fusilli pasta. In a small container, combine the cooking oil and butter and set aside. Set aside ¼ cup of the rice wine.

In a small bowl, combine the Hot Wok Seasonings; set aside. In another small bowl, combine the Hot Wok Sauce ingredients and set aside.

HOT WOK ACTION

Bring at least 4 quarts of water to a vigorous boil. Lightly salt the water and add the pasta. Cook the pasta until it is just cooked and slightly firm to the bite, about 8 minutes. Immediately transfer the pasta to a colander to drain.

Meanwhile, place a wok over the highest heat. When the wok becomes very hot, add the oil and butter to the center. Roll the oil around the wok and when the oil gives off just a wisp of smoke, add the Hot Wok Seasonings. Stir-fry the seasonings, and as soon as they turn white, about 5 seconds, add the mushrooms. Stir and toss the mushrooms until they soften slightly, about 3 minutes. As you stir-fry the mushrooms, add the ¼ cup rice wine, so that the mushrooms soften more quickly and develop a fuller flavor.

Stir in the snow peas and green onions. Continue cooking until the snow peas turn bright green, about 1 minute. Add the cooked pasta. Stir the Hot Wok Sauce, and then pour it into the wok. Stir and toss until all the ingredients are glazed with the sauce. Taste and adjust the seasonings. Immediately transfer the pasta to a heated platter or dinner plates, sprinkle on the toasted pine nuts, and serve.

Because it is difficult to integrate pasta evenly with the vegetables during stir-frying, this pasta recipe recommends tossing the cold cooked pasta with the vegetables in a large bowl as a preliminary step just before beginning to stir-fry. During the final cooking, the noodles reheat, the vegetables turn brightly colored but stay crisp, and the sauce glazes all the ingredients. To achieve a balanced mix and an attractive look, be sure to cut the vegetables into approximately the same shape and size as the pasta.

Thai Primavera with Summer Vegetables

SERVES 6 TO 8 AS A SIDE DISH OR 4 AS THE MAIN ENTRÉE

HOT WOK INGREDIENTS

1 red bell pepper

10 button mushrooms

12 thin asparagus spears

8 baby yellow crookneck squash

1 cup baby string beans

6 ounces dried bowtie pasta

3 tablespoons cooking oil

3 small tomatoes, quartered

1 cup cilantro sprigs

HOT WOK SEASONINGS

1 stem lemon grass, finely minced

4 cloves garlic, finely minced

HOT WOK SAUCE

2 teaspoons finely minced lime zest

3 tablespoons rice wine or dry sherry

3 tablespoons tomato sauce

2 tablespoons freshly squeezed lime juice

2 tablespoons brown sugar

2 tablespoons oyster sauce

1 tablespoon Thai Sriracha chile sauce

2 teaspoons cornstarch

ADVANCE PREPARATION

Discard the stem and seeds from the bell pepper. Cut the pepper into long 1/4-inch-wide strips; then cut the strips into 1 1/2-inch-long pieces. Cut the mushrooms into 1/4-inch-wide slices. Snap off tough asparagus ends. Cut asparagus on a sharp diagonal into 1-inch lengths. Slice the squash. In a bowl, combine the pepper, mushrooms, asparagus, squash, and string beans.

Bring at least 4 quarts of water to a vigorous boil. Lightly salt the water and add the pasta. Cook the pasta until it is al dente, about 6 minutes. Transfer the pasta to a colander to drain. Rinse with cool water, and drain again. Stir in 1 tablespoon of the cooking oil, and refrigerate.

In separate containers, set aside the tomatoes, pasta, remaining cooking oil, and cilantro. In a small container, combine the Hot Wok Seasonings; set aside. In a small bowl, combine the Hot Wok Sauce ingredients and set aside.

HOT WOK ACTION

Coarsely chop the cilantro. Combine the pasta with the bell pepper, mushrooms, asparagus, squash, and string beans, and mix to evenly blend.

Place a wok over the highest heat. When the wok becomes very hot, add the cooking oil to the center. Roll the oil around the wok and when the oil gives off just a wisp of smoke, add the Hot Wok Seasonings. Stir-fry the seasonings, and as soon as they turn white, about 5 seconds, add the vegetable-pasta mix. Stir and toss about 3 minutes.

Add the tomatoes, stirring and tossing with the other ingredients to mix evenly. Stir the Hot Wok Sauce, and then pour it into the wok. Stir and toss until all the ingredients are glazed with the sauce, the pasta is piping hot, and the vegetables brighten, about 2 minutes. Taste and adjust the seasonings. Immediately transfer the pasta to a heated platter or dinner plates, sprinkle on the chopped cilantro, and serve.

Small amounts of left-over barbecued meats, ground sausage, precooked and thinly sliced sausage links, and smoked meats add complex low-note flavors to stir-fry pasta and rice dishes. In this recipe, if you cannot buy small whole smoked chickens (you may have to place a special order with your butcher), substitute ham or a barbecued meat rather than using the inferior-tasting smoked chicken loaf found in many supermarket deli cases.

Jade Pasta with Smoked Chicken and Hazelnuts

SERVES 6 TO 8 AS A SIDE DISH OR 4 AS THE MAIN ENTRÉE

HOT WOK INGREDIENTS

½ smoked chicken (about ½ pound)

¼ pound button mushrooms

4 whole green onions

2 cups fresh bean sprouts, perfectly white

1 cup shelled hazelnuts

6 ounces dried shell-shaped pasta

2 tablespoons cooking oil

HOT WOK SAUCE

3 cloves garlic

1 tablespoon coarsely chopped fresh ginger

½ cup spinach leaves

¼ cup mint leaves

¼ cup cilantro sprigs

10 large basil leaves

½ cup whipping cream

¼ cup rice wine or dry sherry

2 tablespoons thin soy sauce

2 teaspoons hoisin sauce

1 teaspoon sugar

1 teaspoon Asian chile sauce

½ teaspoon salt

ADVANCE PREPARATION

Pull the chicken away from the bones. Discard the skin. Cut the meat into bite-sized pieces and refrigerate.

Preheat the oven to 325°. Cut the mushrooms into ¼-inch-wide pieces. Cut the green onions on a sharp diagonal into 1-inch lengths. In a bowl, combine the mushrooms and green onions, and refrigerate. Set aside the bean sprouts. Place the hazelnuts on a baking sheet, and bake in the preheated oven until lightly golden, about 15 minutes. Remove from the oven, and if the hazelnuts still have their skins attached, rub the nuts vigorously between your palms to loosen and remove the skins. Set aside the nuts at room temperature. In separate containers, set aside the pasta and cooking oil.

Place all the Hot Wok Sauce ingredients in an electric blender. Blend into a liquid and refrigerate.

HOT WOK ACTION

Bring at least 4 quarts of water to a vigorous boil. Lightly salt the water and add the pasta. Cook the pasta until it is just cooked and slightly firm to the bite, about 8 minutes. Immediately drain in a colander.

Meanwhile, place a wok over the highest heat. When the wok becomes very hot, add the cooking oil. Roll the oil around the wok and when the oil gives off just a wisp of smoke, add all the vegetables except the bean sprouts. Stir and toss the vegetables until the green onions turn bright green, about 2 minutes.

Stir the Hot Wok Sauce, and then pour it into the wok. Stir in the pasta, smoked chicken, and hazelnuts. Stir and toss until all the ingredients are glazed with the sauce. Taste and adjust the seasonings. Immediately transfer the pasta to a heated platter or dinner plates and serve.

B owtie pasta creates a whimsical look when juxtaposed with slivered red bell pepper, asparagus tips, and tender white corn kernels. The small center pleats of the pasta capture the rich chipotle chile sauce infused with its underlying flavors of orange, garlic, tomatoes, and cinnamon. A final sprinkling of goat cheese adds color contrast and an intriguing creaminess.

Hot Southwest Pasta with Chipotle Chiles

SERVES 6 TO 8 AS A SIDE DISH OR 4 AS THE MAIN ENTRÉE

HOT WOK INGREDIENTS

1 red bell pepper

2 ears white corn

¼ pound Chinese long beans

½ cup cilantro sprigs

1 ounce soft goat cheese, crumbled

6 ounces dried bowtie pasta

2 tablespoons cooking oil

HOT WOK SEASONINGS

4 cloves garlic, finely minced

2 shallots, minced

HOT WOK SAUCE

3 vine-ripened tomatoes

1½ tablespoons canned chipotle chiles in adobo sauce

⅓ cup orange juice, freshly squeezed

2 tablespoons white wine vinegar

2 tablespoons brown sugar

2 tablespoons thin soy sauce

2 teaspoons cornstarch

½ teaspoon salt

¼ teaspoon cinnamon

⅛ teaspoon allspice

ADVANCE PREPARATION

Discard the stem and seeds from the bell pepper. Cut pepper into ½-inch-wide strips, and then cut the strips into 1-inch lengths. Cut the kernels off the ears of corn. Cut the long beans on a sharp diagonal into 1-inch lengths.

In a bowl, combine the pepper, corn, and long beans, and refrigerate. In separate containers, set aside the cilantro, crumbled goat cheese, pasta, and cooking oil.

In a small container, combine the Hot Wok Seasonings; set aside. To prepare the Hot Wok Sauce, discard the stems and seeds from the tomatoes. In a food processor, mince the tomatoes. Transfer the tomatoes to a bowl. Place the chipotle chiles in adobo sauce in an electric blender and liquefy, or mince finely by hand. Add the chile mixture and remaining sauce ingredients to the bowl of tomatoes, and refrigerate.

HOT WOK ACTION

Coarsely chop the cilantro. Bring at least 4 quarts of water to a vigorous boil. Lightly salt the water and add the pasta. Cook the pasta until it is just cooked and slightly firm to the bite, about 8 minutes. Transfer to a colander and drain.

Meanwhile, place a wok over the highest heat. When the wok becomes very hot, add the cooking oil to the center. Roll the oil around the wok and when the oil gives off just a wisp of smoke, add the Hot Wok Seasonings. Stir-fry the seasonings, and as soon as they turn white, about 5 seconds, add the vegetables. Stir and toss the vegetables until the red peppers brighten, about 2 minutes.

Add the pasta to the wok. Stir the Hot Wok Sauce, and then pour it into the wok. Stir and toss until all the ingredients are glazed with the sauce, about 1 minute. Stir in the cilantro. Taste and adjust the seasonings. Immediately transfer the pasta to a heated platter or dinner plates, sprinkle with goat cheese, and serve.

Coconut, curry, chiles and fresh herbs form a classic partnership in Thai cooking to flavor sautéed shrimp, long-simmering meats, and stir-fry noodle dishes. Among the many flavor modifications, you can delete the curry powder or substitute 2 teaspoons of a homemade Thai curry paste, omit the chile sauce, replace the fish sauce with an equal amount of oyster sauce, or exchange fresh cilantro for the mint and basil. Try adding ³/₄ pound boned and marinated duck meat that is seared in the wok briefly, set aside while stir-frying the pasta, and then returned to the wok for a few seconds to combine evenly with all the other ingredients. Fantastic!

Curried Coconut Noodles with Mint and Basil

SERVES 6 TO 8 AS A SIDE DISH OR 4 AS THE MAIN ENTRÉE

HOT WOK INGREDIENTS

1 head broccoli

2 cups snow peas

¼ small purple cabbage

½ pound small button mushrooms

½ cup raw peanuts

½ cup cooking oil

2 limes

6 ounces corkscrew or penne pasta

HOT WOK SEASONINGS

3 shallots, minced

4 cloves garlic, finely minced

2 tablespoons very finely minced fresh
    ginger

HOT WOK SAUCE

½ cup coconut milk

¼ cup rice wine or dry sherry

2 tablespoons fish sauce

1 tablespoon hoisin sauce

2 teaspoons curry powder

2 teaspoons cornstarch

1 teaspoon Asian chile sauce

¼ cup chopped mint leaves

¼ cup chopped basil leaves

ADVANCE PREPARATION

Cut the broccoli flowers off the stem, cutting the large ones in half. Discard the broccoli stems. Place the broccoli in a single layer on a dinner plate, cover with plastic wrap, and microwave on high for 1 minute at a time, until the broccoli brightens in color. Or, stir the broccoli into 2 quarts of boiling water. As soon as the broccoli brightens in color, about 1 minute, immediately transfer it to a bowl filled with cold water and ice. When the broccoli is thoroughly chilled, remove the broccoli from the ice water and pat dry. Snap the stem ends from the snow peas and pull the stems along the top ridge to remove any fiber. Cut cabbage into ½-inch-wide and 2-inch-long pieces. Thinly slice the mushrooms. In a bowl, combine all the vegetables and refrigerate.

Place the peanuts and cooking oil in a small saucepan and put over medium-high heat. Stir the peanuts until they turn a very light golden, and then immediately transfer the nuts and oil to a sieve placed over a heat-proof bowl. Cool the peanuts and then set aside at room temperature. In a small container, reserve 2 tablespoons of the cooking oil for stir-frying. Cut the limes into thin wedges and set aside. Set aside the pasta.

In a small container, combine the Hot Wok Seasonings; set aside. In a small bowl, combine the Hot Wok Sauce ingredients and set aside.

HOT WOK ACTION

Bring at least 4 quarts of water to a vigorous boil. Lightly salt the water and add the pasta. Cook the pasta until it is just cooked and slightly firm to the bite, about 8 minutes. Transfer the pasta to a colander to drain.

Meanwhile, place a wok over the highest heat. When the wok becomes very hot, add the cooking oil to the center. Roll the oil around the wok and when the oil gives off just a wisp of smoke, add the Hot Wok Seasonings. Stir-fry the seasonings, and as soon as they turn white, about 5 seconds, add all the vegetables. Stir and toss the vegetables until the snow peas turn bright green, about 2 minutes.

Add the pasta and stir and toss with the other ingredients to mix evenly. Stir the Hot Wok Sauce, and then pour it into the wok. Add the peanuts. Stir and toss until all the ingredients are glazed with the sauce, about 2 minutes. Taste and adjust the seasonings. Immediately transfer the pasta to a heated platter or dinner plates and serve, accompanied by lime wedges.

ost of the recipes in this book that use pasta call for cooking it at the last minute. However, as long as you choose a dried pasta that takes at least 5 minutes to cook, you can simplify the last-minute preparation by pre-cooking the pasta. First, boil the pasta until nearly cooked, then drain the pasta, rinse under cold water to arrest the cooking process, drain again, and as a final step, stir in about one tablespoon of tasteless cooking oil to prevent the pasta from sticking together. Refrigerate the pasta until ready to complete the stir-fry steps.

Salmon-Pasta Stir-Fry

SERVES 4 AS THE MAIN ENTRÉE

HOT WOK INGREDIENTS

1 salmon fillet, skinned and pin bones removed (1 pound)

1 tablespoon thin soy sauce

1 tablespoon rice wine or dry sherry

2 teaspoons plus 3 tablespoons cooking oil

3 ears tender white corn

¼ pound thin-stemmed asparagus

1 red bell pepper

2 bunches chives

1½ cups large pecans

6 ounces corkscrew pasta

HOT WOK SEASONINGS

2 cloves garlic, finely minced

2 tablespoons very finely minced fresh ginger

HOT WOK SAUCE

2 teaspoons orange zest

½ cup orange juice, freshly squeezed

¼ cup rice wine or dry sherry

3 tablespoons oyster sauce

2 tablespoons dark sesame oil

1 tablespoon cornstarch

1 teaspoon sugar

1 teaspoon Asian chile sauce

ADVANCE PREPARATION

Preheat the oven to 325°. Cut the salmon in half lengthwise. Cut across the salmon, making ¼-inch-wide pieces. In a small bowl, combine the soy sauce, rice wine, and 2 teaspoons cooking oil. Mix thoroughly with the salmon. Marinate the salmon at least 15 minutes but not longer than 8 hours, refrigerated.

Cut the kernels off the corn. Cut the asparagus on a sharp diagonal into 1-inch lengths. Seed and stem the bell pepper, then cut into matchstick-size pieces. Combine the corn, asparagus, and pepper, and then refrigerate. Cut the chives on a diagonal into 1-inch lengths. Place the pecans on a cookie sheet and toast in the preheated oven for 15 minutes; then set aside. Set aside separately the pasta. Divide the cooking oil in half and set aside in small containers.

In a small bowl, combine the Hot Wok Seasonings; set aside. In another small bowl, combine the Hot Wok Sauce ingredients and refrigerate.

HOT WOK ACTION

Bring at least 4 quarts of water to a vigorous boil. Lightly salt the water and add the pasta. Cook the pasta until it is just cooked and slightly firm to the bite, about 8 minutes. Transfer to a colander and drain.

Place a wok over the highest heat. When the wok becomes very hot, add half the cooking oil to the center. Roll the oil around the wok and when the oil gives off just a wisp of smoke, add the salmon. Stir and toss the salmon until it loses its raw exterior color, about 2 minutes, and then slide the salmon onto a plate.

Immediately return the wok to the highest heat. Add the remaining cooking oil and the Hot Wok Seasonings. Stir-fry the seasonings, and as soon as they turn white, about 5 seconds, add the vegetables. Stir and toss the vegetables until the pepper brightens in color, about 2 minutes.

Stir the Hot Wok Sauce, and then pour it into the wok. Return the salmon to the wok and add the pasta and pecans. Stir and toss until all the ingredients are glazed with the sauce, about 2 minutes. Stir in the chives.

Taste and adjust the seasonings. Immediately transfer the pasta to a heated platter or dinner plates and serve.

To create your own fried-rice recipes, prepare 4 cups of cold, cooked rice, and 2 cups of diced vegetables that provide a colorful contrast. For non-vegetarian fried rice, set aside up to ½ pound diced raw shrimp, raw marinated meat, or 4 beaten eggs. Then choose one of the Hot Wok Seasonings and Hot Wok Sauces from any recipe in this book. Follow the instructions given for Hot Wok Action in this recipe. Cold cooked meat or seafood, such as crab meat or barbecued chicken from last night's dinner, should be stirred into the fried rice at the very end of cooking just so it can reheat.

Thai Fried Rice with Coconut Herb Sauce

SERVES 4 AS THE MAIN ENTRÉE

HOT WOK INGREDIENTS

3 chicken breast halves, boned and
   skinned, about ½ pound
1 green bell pepper
2 small Japanese eggplant
2 vine-ripened tomatoes
4 whole green onions
3 tablespoons cooking oil
4 cups cold cooked white rice (page 97)
¼ cup rice wine or dry sherry

HOT WOK SEASONINGS

3 cloves garlic, finely minced
1 tablespoon finely minced fresh lemon
   grass

HOT WOK SAUCE

¼ cup coconut milk
¼ cup orange juice, freshly squeezed
2 tablespoons rice wine or dry sherry
2 tablespoons oyster sauce
3 fresh serrano chiles, including seeds,
   finely minced
¼ cup chopped mint leaves
¼ cup chopped cilantro

ADVANCE PREPARATION

Cut the chicken into ¼-inch-thick strips, then cut across the strips to make ¼-inch cubes. Place the chicken in a small bowl.

Discard the stem and seeds from the pepper, then cut the pepper into ¼-inch cubes. Cut the eggplant into ¼-inch slices; cut the slices into ¼-inch-wide strips and then cut the strips into ¼-inch cubes. Cut the tomatoes in half, squeeze out their seeds, then cut the halves into bite-sized wedges. Cut the green onions on a sharp diagonal into ¼-inch-long pieces. Place all the vegetables in a bowl, and refrigerate. Divide the cooking oil in half and set aside in small containers. Place the cold cooked rice in a plastic bag and squeeze the bag with your fingers to separate the rice into individual grains. Set aside the ¼ cup rice wine.

In a small container, combine the Hot Wok Seasonings and set aside. In a separate bowl, combine the Hot Wok Sauce ingredients. Add 3 tablespoons of the Hot Wok Sauce to the chicken, mix to combine evenly, and then refrigerate the chicken. Set aside the remaining Hot Wok Sauce.

HOT WOK ACTION

Place a wok over the highest heat. When the wok is very hot, add half the cooking oil to the center. Roll the oil around the sides of the wok and when the oil just begins to give off a wisp of smoke, add the chicken. Stir and toss until the chicken loses its raw exterior color, about 2 minutes, and then slide the chicken onto a plate.

Immediately return the wok to the highest heat. Add the remaining cooking oil and the Hot Wok Seasonings. Stir-fry the seasonings, and as soon as they turn white, about 5 seconds, add the vegetables. Stir and toss the vegetables until the green onions brighten in color and the eggplant soften, about 1 minute. During cooking, add the ¼ cup rice wine to moisten the eggplant.

Add the cold cooked rice to the wok. Stir and toss to evenly mix all the ingredients, and then add the Hot Wok Sauce. Stir and toss until the rice is thoroughly reheated, about 3 minutes. Return the chicken to the wok and mix to combine evenly. Taste and adjust the seasonings. Immediately transfer the stir-fry to a heated platter or dinner plates and serve.

Wild Rice with Shrimp and Crab

We remain unenthusiastic about brown rice, regardless of its nutritional value, because its taste overwhelms most ingredients in fried-rice recipes. On the other hand, wild rice (which is a grass and not botanically related to rice) adds an exotic, resilient texture and nutty taste when substituted for white rice in all fried-rice recipes. (You may also use a packaged rice mix that includes wild rice.) You will need 3 cups of cold cooked wild rice in this recipe. Bring 2 quarts of water to a vigorous boil, add 1 cup of rinsed wild rice, season with a little salt, and simmer for approximately 45 minutes or until three-quarters of the rice grains have puffed. Immediately transfer the wild rice to a colander, rinse with cold water to chill, drain thoroughly, and refrigerate. Cooked wild rice can be refrigerated for up to 10 days.

SERVES 4 AS THE MAIN ENTRÉE

HOT WOK INGREDIENTS

½ pound medium-sized raw shrimp

½ pound fresh crab meat

2 whole green onions

1 cup freshly shelled peas, or snow peas

3 ounces enoki mushrooms

½ cup fresh cilantro sprigs

⅓ cup pine nuts

3 cups cold cooked wild rice

2 tablespoons cooking oil

2 tablespoons unsalted butter

¼ cup water

HOT WOK SEASONING

2 tablespoons very finely minced fresh ginger

HOT WOK SAUCE

¼ cup port

1 tablespoon thin soy sauce

2 tablespoons oyster sauce

2 tablespoons dark sesame oil

1 tablespoon red wine vinegar

1 teaspoon cornstarch

½ teaspoon Asian chile sauce

ADVANCE PREPARATION

Preheat the oven to 325°. Shell and devein the shrimp, then cut them deeply lengthwise and refrigerate. Discard any shells from the crab meat, and then refrigerate the crab. Cut the green onions on a sharp diagonal into ¼-inch-thick slivers. Combine the peas and green onions in a small bowl and refrigerate. Discard the root ends from the enoki mushrooms and pull apart their stems. In separate containers, set aside the mushrooms and cilantro sprigs.

Toast the pine nuts in the preheated oven until they become golden, about 8 minutes. Set aside the cooked wild rice. In small containers, set aside the cooking oil and the butter. Set aside the ¼ cup water.

In a small container, set aside the Hot Wok Seasoning. In a small bowl, combine the Hot Wok Sauce ingredients and set aside.

HOT WOK ACTION

Chop the cilantro. Place a wok over the highest heat. When the wok becomes very hot, add the cooking oil to the center. Roll the oil around the wok and when the oil gives off just a wisp of smoke, add the shrimp. Stir and toss the shrimp until it loses its raw outside color, about 2 minutes, and then slide the shrimp onto a plate.

Immediately return the wok to the highest heat. Add the butter and the Hot Wok Seasoning. As soon as the butter melts, add the peas and green onions to the wok. Stir and toss, adding the water so that the peas cook evenly, do not scorch, and turn bright green, about 2 minutes.

Add the wild rice, enoki mushrooms, pine nuts, crab meat, and shrimp to the wok. Stir and toss to combine evenly, and then add the Hot Wok Sauce. Stir and toss until the wild rice is thoroughly reheated, about 3 minutes. Stir in the cilantro. Taste and adjust the seasonings. Immediately transfer the stir-fry to a heated platter or dinner plates and serve.

Successful fried rice depends on using cold, cooked rice because hot rice added to a wok quickly becomes mushy. Cook the rice at least 4 hours before making fried rice and once the rice has cooled, transfer it to a plastic bag and then massage the bag to separate the rice into individual grains. Small clumps do not matter at this stage because these will break apart during the stir-fry process. In case the fried-rice monster attacks, stockpile cooked rice in the refrigerator for up to a week or freeze the rice indefinitely.

California Citrus Fried Rice

SERVES 4 TO 6 AS A SIDE DISH

HOT WOK INGREDIENTS

4 eggs

½ cup currants

1 red bell pepper, cut into ¼-inch cubes

2 small carrots, cut on a sharp diagonal

4 whole green onions, cut on the diagonal

10 stalks asparagus

4 cups cold cooked rice (page 97)

¼ cup white sesame seeds

3 tablespoons cooking oil

¼ cup rice wine or dry sherry

HOT WOK SEASONINGS

3 cloves garlic, finely minced

2 shallots, minced

HOT WOK SAUCE

2 teaspoons minced orange zest

⅓ cup orange juice, freshly squeezed

2 tablespoons rice wine or dry sherry

3 tablespoons oyster sauce

2 tablespoons dark sesame oil

½ teaspoon Asian chile sauce

ADVANCE PREPARATION

In a small bowl, beat the eggs with a fork and then refrigerate. Place the currants in a small bowl, and cover with hot water for 20 minutes. Then drain and discard the water. Combine the currants, bell pepper, carrots, and green onions. Snap off and discard the tough asparagus ends. Cut the asparagus on a sharp diagonal into ⅛-inch-thick pieces and combine with the other vegetables and refrigerate.

Place the cold cooked rice in a plastic bag and squeeze the bag with your fingers to separate the rice into individual grains; set aside. Place the sesame seeds in a small, ungreased sauté pan, and toast them over medium heat until they turn light golden; set the sesame seeds aside. Divide the cooking oil, putting 1 tablespoon in a small container and 2 tablespoons in another. Set aside the ¼ cup rice wine.

In a small bowl, combine the Hot Wok Seasonings; set aside. In a small bowl, combine the Hot Wok Sauce ingredients.

HOT WOK ACTION

Place a wok over the highest heat. When the wok becomes very hot, add 1 tablespoon of the cooking oil to the center. Roll the oil around the wok and when the oil gives off just a wisp of smoke, add the eggs. Stir and toss the eggs until they become lightly scrambled, then immediately slide the eggs onto a plate.

Immediately return the wok to the highest heat. Add the remaining cooking oil and the Hot Wok Seasonings. Stir-fry the seasonings, and as soon as they turn white, about 5 seconds, add the vegetables. Stir and toss the vegetables until the asparagus and carrots brighten in color, about 3 minutes. During this cooking, add the ¼ cup rice wine to prevent the vegetables from becoming scorched.

Then add the rice, and return the scrambled eggs to the wok. Stir the Hot Wok Sauce, and then add it and the sesame seeds to the wok. Stir and toss until all the ingredients are mixed evenly, and the rice is thoroughly reheated, about 3 minutes. Taste and adjust the seasonings. Immediately transfer the stir-fry to a heated platter or dinner plates and serve.

Never use instant rice. Good fried rice depends on using the best rice such as California or Texas long-grain white rice, Indian basmati rice, or Thai jasmine rice. To cook, place 1 cup white rice in a small sieve and rinse with cold water to remove the gluten and starch. Rinse until the water becomes clear, then transfer the rice to a small saucepan. Placing your index fingertip on the top of the rice, add just enough water so it rises to the knuckle line closest to your index fingertip. Bring the water to a vigorous boil over medium heat, and when the water just begins to disappear and the rice has little craters across the surface, cover the saucepan, reduce to a simmer, and cook 15 more minutes. Once the rice is cooked, cool and transfer it to the refrigerator.

Southwest Fried Rice with Ancho Chiles

SERVES 4 TO 6 AS A SIDE DISH

HOT WOK INGREDIENTS

4 eggs

1 red bell pepper

1 zucchini

2 ears white corn

4 whole green onions

1 cup pecan halves

4 cups cold cooked white rice

3 tablespoons cooking oil

½ cup cilantro

HOT WOK SEASONING

3 cloves garlic, finely minced

HOT WOK SAUCE

2 dried ancho chiles

⅓ cup tomato sauce

¼ cup rice wine or dry sherry

3 tablespoons oyster sauce

2 tablespoons dark sesame oil

1 tablespoon brown sugar

1 tablespoon white wine vinegar

2 teaspoons Southwest-style or Asian
   chile sauce

ADVANCE PREPARATION

Preheat the oven to 325°. In a small bowl, beat the eggs with a fork and refrigerate. Discard the seeds and stem from the bell pepper, and then cut the pepper into ¼-inch cubes.

Discard the stem ends from the zucchini, and then cut the zucchini on a sharp diagonal into ¼-inch-thick slices. Overlap the zucchini slices and cut into ¼-inch matchstick pieces; place the pieces together, and cut into ¼-inch cubes. Discard the corn husks, and cut the kernels off the cob. Cut the green onions on a sharp diagonal into ¼-inch-long pieces. In a small bowl, combine all the vegetables and refrigerate.

Toast the pecans in the preheated oven for 15 minutes, and then set aside. Place the cold cooked rice in a plastic bag and squeeze the bag with your fingers to separate the rice into individual grains. Divide the cooking oil, putting 1 tablespoon in one small container and 2 tablespoons in another. Set aside the cilantro.

In a small container, set aside the garlic. Place the ancho chiles in a small bowl and cover the chiles with boiling water. When the chiles soften, mince the chiles finely. In a small bowl, combine the minced chiles with the remaining Hot Wok Sauce ingredients.

HOT WOK ACTION

Chop the fresh cilantro and set aside. Place a wok over the highest heat. When the wok becomes very hot, add 1 tablespoon of the cooking oil to the center. Roll the oil around the wok and when the oil gives off just a wisp of smoke, add the eggs. Stir and toss the eggs until they are softly scrambled, and then slide them onto a plate.

Immediately return the wok to the highest heat. Add the remaining cooking oil and the garlic. Stir-fry the garlic, and as soon as it turns white, about 5 seconds, add the vegetables. Stir and toss the vegetables until the peppers brighten, about 1 minute. Add the rice. Stir and toss the rice for 1 minute.

Stir the Hot Wok Sauce. Add the sauce, scrambled eggs, and pecans to the wok. Stir and toss all the ingredients until they are mixed evenly and the rice is thoroughly reheated, about 3 minutes. Stir in the cilantro. Taste and adjust the seasonings. Immediately transfer the stir-fry to a heated platter or dinner plates and serve.

Hot Wok Troubleshooting

If you have encountered difficulties with wok cooking, take this open-book quiz and discover the answers you've been looking for. Refer to pages 5 to 6 (Hot Fire, Hot Wok, Hot Action) for more detailed explanations.

Was it difficult to stir-fry and read the cooking directions simultaneously? Just line up the ingredients next to the stove in the order they go into the wok, and close the cookbook (see Hot Wok Preparation, 3 and 5 and Hot Wok Stir-Fry, 3).

Did the wok fail to make a sizzling noise when you added ingredients? The wok was not properly preheated (see Hot Wok Heat, 1), and/or the burner was not on the highest setting throughout the stir-fry process (see Hot Wok Heat, 2), and/or too large a quantity of meat, seafood, or vegetables were stir-fried (see Hot Wok Preparation, 4).

Did the oil smoke heavily or burst into flames? The wrong oil was added (see Hot Wok Oil, 1) and/or the oil was added too slowly to the preheated wok (see Hot Wok Oil, 2), and/or the main ingredients were not added to the wok the moment the oil began to give off a wisp of smoke (see Hot Wok Oil, 3).

Did the oil splatter? Excess marinade was not drained from the meat, or the shrimp or scallops were not dried with paper towels, or the vegetables were still moist (see Hot Wok Action, 1).

Did the Hot Wok Seasonings burn? Within seconds after the Hot Wok Seasonings enter the wok, add the next main ingredient (see Hot Wok Stir-Fry, 4).

Did the meat or seafood stick to the sides of the wok? The wok was not properly preheated (see Hot Wok Heat, 1), and/or there was too little oil used for stir-frying (see Hot Wok Oil, 2), and/or the food was not stirred and tossed frequently (see Hot Wok Stir-Frying, 2), and/or the wok was not properly seasoned (see Hot Wok Equipment, page 3).

Were the meat, seafood, or vegetables raw? The food was cut too large (see Hot Wok Preparation, 1), and/or the food was not stir-fried until it brightened (see Hot Wok Stir-Frying, 3).

Were the main ingredients overcooked? Judge the cooking time by the change of color (see Hot Wok Stir-Frying 3), and exaggerate by undercooking the food (see Hot Wok Stir-Frying, 5).

Was the sauce watery? Always have a cornstarch mixture prepared in order to thicken a watery sauce (see Hot Wok Finishing Touches, 1).

Were you dissatisfied with the taste of the dish? As the final step, always taste and adjust the seasonings (see Hot Wok Finishing Touches, 2).

Was it difficult to transfer the stir-fry from the wok to the serving platter or dinner plates? Always give the wok a vigorous shake and then immediately tip the wok toward you in order to slide the food out of the wok (see Hot Wok Finishing Touches, 3).

Was the stir-fry dish no longer piping hot when served? Serve every stir-fry dish immediately after cooking (see Hot Wok Finishing Touches, 4).

Glossary of Ingredients

CHILES, FRESH: The smaller the chile, the spicier its taste. More than 80 percent of the heat is concentrated in the inside ribbing and seeds. To use, discard the stem, and then mince the chile (without removing the seeds) in an electric mini-chopper.

CHILE SAUCE, ASIAN: This is a general term for the many Asian chile sauces, labeled as "chile paste," "chile sauce," and "chile paste with garlic." Best brand: Rooster Delicious Hot Chile Garlic Sauce, sold in 8-ounce clear plastic jars with a green cap. Refrigerate after opening.

CHILE SAUCE, THAI SRIRACHA: This is an orange-colored, mild chile sauce that is manufactured in Thailand and sold under the Swan brand name. Don't confuse this with the very spicy sriracha sauces manufactured in Hong Kong and the United States. Refrigerate after opening.

COCONUT MILK: Used to add flavor and body to stir-fry sauces. Always purchase a Thai brand that contains only coconut and water. Stir the coconut milk before using. Best brand: Chaokoh brand from Thailand. Once opened, coconut milk is perishable and should be refrigerated no longer than one week.

COOKING OIL: Refers to any tasteless oil that has a high smoking temperature, such as peanut oil, canola oil, safflower oil, and corn oil.

CURRY POWDER AND PASTE: Curry powder is a blend of many spices. Curry paste is a blend of spices mashed into a paste with oil. Curry paste has a much more complex flavor than curry powder. For every 1 tablespoon of curry powder, use 1 teaspoon of the curry paste. Best brand: Madras Indian Curry Paste, which is sold in most supermarkets.

FISH SAUCE: Fish sauce, which is made from fermenting anchovies or other fish in a brine, is used in Thai and Vietnamese cooking the way the Chinese use soy sauce. Always buy Thai fish sauce, which has the lowest salt content. Never use fish stock or bouillon as a substitute because the taste is completely different. Once opened, fish sauce lasts indefinitely at room temperature. Best brands: Three Crab brand or Tiparos Fish Sauce.

GINGER, FRESH: These pungent, spicy, knobby brown "roots" are sold in the produce section of all supermarkets. Buy firm ginger with smooth skin. It is unnecessary to peel ginger unless the skin is wrinkled. To use: cut the ginger crosswise into paper-thin slices, then very finely mince in an electric mini-food processor. Store ginger root in the refrigerator or at room temperature. There is no substitute for fresh ginger.

HOISIN SAUCE: Hoisin sauce, a thick and sweet, spicy, dark condiment, is made with soy beans, chiles, garlic, ginger, and sugar. Once opened, it keeps indefinitely at room temperature. Best brand: Koon Chun Hoisin Sauce.

LEMON GRASS: Lemon grass has an 8-inch-long woody stem and long slender green leaves. Buy lemon grass that has firm, smooth stems and green leaves without any brown edges. Finely mince the center section of the stem, and add it to any stir-fry dish at the same time you add the Hot Wok Seasonings. Because lemon grass quickly loses its flavor a few days after being picked, it is best picked fresh from the garden and used that day. You can substitute ½ teaspoon lemon zest, though the flavor is not quite the same. Never substitute dried or frozen lemon grass, which has no taste.

MUSHROOMS, DRIED CHINESE: A variety of fresh shiitake mushrooms are available dried. Or, if these are unavailable, dried European mushrooms can be substituted. To use, cover with hot water and soak about 30 minutes until the mushrooms soften. Then discard the stems, and cut the mushrooms into bite-sized pieces.

OYSTER SAUCE: Also called "oyster-flavored sauce," this ingredient gives dishes a rich taste without a hint of its seafood origins. A pinch of sugar is usually added to dishes using oyster sauce to counteract its slightly salty taste. Keeps indefinitely in the refrigerator. There is no substitute. Best brands: Sa Cheng Oyster-Flavored Sauce, Hop Sing Lung Oyster Sauce, Factory Oyster-Flavored Sauce, and Lee Kum Kee Oyster-Flavored Sauce, Premium Brand.

PLUM SAUCE: Made with plums, apricots, garlic, red chiles, sugar, vinegar, salt, and water, plum sauce is available at most supermarkets. Once opened, it lasts indefinitely if refrigerated. Best brand: Koon Chun Plum Sauce.

RICE STICKS: These are long, thin, dried rice-starch vermicelli. Rice sticks dropped into hot oil instantly puff into a huge white mass many times their original size. They are available at most supermarkets and all Asian markets. They will last indefinitely at room temperature. Always purchase Sailing Boat Brand Rice Sticks, sold in 1-pound packages.

RICE WINE OR DRY SHERRY: Always use good quality dry sherry or rice wine, such as Pagoda's Shao Xing Rice Wine, or Pagoda Shao Hsing Hua Tiao Chiew.

SESAME OIL, DARK: This is a nutty, dark golden brown oil made from toasted, crushed sesame seeds. Do not confuse dark sesame oil with the clear-colored sesame oil that has no flavor or with "black" sesame oil, which has far too strong a taste. Dark sesame oil is used just to add flavor to stir-fry dishes and never as a cooking oil because it smokes at a very low temperature. Dark sesame oil will last for at least a year at room temperature, and indefinitely in the refrigerator. Best brand: Kadoya Sesame Oil.

SOY SAUCE, THIN: "Thin" or "light" soy sauce is a mildly salty liquid made from soy beans, roasted wheat, yeast, and salt and should not be confused with the inferior-tasting low-sodium brands. Once opened it lasts indefinitely at room temperature. Best brands: Pearl River Bridge Golden Label Superior Soya Sauce, Koon Chun Thin Soy Sauce, or Kikkoman Regular Soy Sauce.

SOY SAUCE, HEAVY: "Heavy," "dark," or "black" soy sauce is thin soy sauce, plus the addition of molasses or caramel, and is used to add a richer flavor and color to sauces, stews, and curries. Never confuse heavy soy sauce with "thick" soy sauce sold in jars, which is a syrup-like molasses. Once opened, heavy soy sauce keeps indefinitely at room temperature. Best brand: Pearl River Bridge Mushroom Soy Sauce.

SZECHWAN PEPPERCORNS: These are small reddish brown seeds, all partly opened, that have a beautiful aromatic flavor without the spice of black or white peppercorns. They are available at all Asian markets. To use, toast Szechwan peppercorns in a grease-free sauté pan just until they smoke, grind in an electric spice grinder, and then sift the ground pepper to remove the brown exterior shells. Store ground Szechwan peppercorns as you would other spices (for no longer than 6 months).

TAMARIND: Tamarind, which is from pods that grow on tamarind trees in the tropics, has a fruity, sour taste. Tamarind is usually sold in 8-ounce and 1-pound blocks at all Asian markets. Break off a thumb-sized piece of pulp, add just enough hot water to cover the tamarind, and then after 10 minutes when the pulp softens, rub the pulp with your fingers in order to extract all of its flavor; then strain the liquid through the sieve and discard remaining pulp. Tamarind pulp will last indefinitely if stored in a cool, dark pantry.

WRAPPERS, MU SHU: These are 6- to 8-inch-diameter tortilla-like wraps that are sold frozen in all Asian markets. To use, thaw and then reheat in the microwave oven, or wrap in aluminum foil and warm for 10 minutes in a 325° oven.

Acknowledgments

This cookbook would not have been possible without Phil Wood, who as our publisher and friend, offered enthusiastic encouragement and sage advice throughout the birth of the book. Other key people at Ten Speed Press were Jo Ann Deck, who embraced our proposal from the outset; Kirsty Melville, who as our editor skillfully guided the proposal from a rough outline to this finished book; and Lorena Jones, whose inspired editing and insights improved the text at every juncture. We've enjoyed the many hours spent poring over the book's layout with our friend and book designer Beverly Wilson. Her design talent, creativity and laughter were a wonderful addition to our team. Thanks for sharing our vision.

We found rich sources for props and the beautiful ceramic art. Many thanks to the dedicated tabletop-art galleries: Karla Clement and Sharreen Azevedo of Out of Hand Gallery, San Francisco; and to Margo and Sally Tantau of Tantau gallery, St. Helena, for providing the unique artist-made dishes for the photography.

Many friends helped bring this book into print and we are deeply appreciative for your support. Jack and Dolores Cakebread provided their winery kitchen for testing many of these recipes with a small group of cooking friends. Bettylu Kessler helped with key aspects of completing the manuscript and testing the recipes. Sandy Davison's food styling skills gave these photographs a beautiful sense of realism. Susan Grode, our attorney, helped refine our book proposal and offered continued support.

After the recipes were tested at our home and used in cooking classes, they were given a final evaluation by the following home cooks. This book gained much from your special insights. Thank you Florence Antico, Kathy Bergin and David Lampkin, Ginny Bogart, Jo Bowen, Jane Breed, Judy Burnstein, Lynda and Bill Casper, Megan and David Cornhill, Kris Cox, Claire Dishman, Judy Dubrawski, Cary and Kim Feibleman, Peter Feit, Suzanne Figi, Sharie and Ron Goldfarb, Robert Gordon, Blanch and Sy Gottlieb, Donna Hodgens, Linda and Ron Johnson, Bettylu Kessler, Betty Mandrow, Jeremy Mann, Cynthia McMurray, Patricia Niedfelt, Michele Nipper, Erin O'Connor, and Ursula Samaha, Kathleen Sands, Mary Jo and Paul Shane, Ellie Shulman, Karen Sickels, Betty Silbart, Barbara and Scott Smith, Phil Stafford, and Sue Zubik.

Conversion Charts

LIQUID MEASUREMENTS

Cups and Spoons	Liquid Ounces	Approximate Metric Term	Approximate Centiliters	Actual Mililiters
1 tsp	⅙ oz	1 tsp	½ cL	5 mL
1 Tb	½ oz	1 Tb	1 ½ cL	15 mL
¼ c; 4 Tb	2 oz	½ dL; 4 Tb	6 cL	59 mL
⅓ c; 5 Tb	2 ⅔ oz	¾ dL; 5 Tb	8 cL	79 mL
½ c	4 oz	1 dL	12 cL	119 mL
⅔ c	5 ⅓ oz	1 ½ dL	15 cL	157 mL
¾ c	6 oz	1 ¾ dL	18 cL	178 mL
1 c	8 oz	¼ L	24 cL	237 mL
1 ¼ c	10 oz	3 dL	30 cL	296 mL
1 ⅓ c	10 ⅔ oz	3 ¼ dL	33 cL	325 mL
1 ½ c	12 oz	3 ½ dL	35 cL	355 mL
1 ⅔ c	13 ⅓ oz	3 ¾ dL	39 cL	385 mL
1 ¾ c	14 oz	4 dL	41 cL	414 mL
2 c; 1 pt	16 oz	½ L	47 cL	473 mL
2 ½ c	20 oz	6 dL	60 cL	592 mL
3 c	24 oz	¾ L	70 cL	710 mL
3 ½ c	28 oz	⅘ L; 8 dL	83 cL	829 mL
4 c; 1 qt	32 oz	1 L	95 cL	946 mL
5 c	40 oz	1 ¼ L	113 cL	1134 mL
6 c; 1 ½ qt	48 oz	1 ½ L	142 cL	1420 mL
8 c; 2 qt	64 oz	2 L	190 cL	1893 mL
10 c; 2 ½ qt	80 oz	2 ½ L	235 cL	2366 mL
12 c; 3 qt	96 oz	2 ¾ L	284 cL	2839 mL
4 qt	128 oz	3 ¾ L	375 cL	3785 mL
5 qt	4 ¾ L			
6 qt	5 ½ L (or 6 L)			
8 qt	7 ½ (or 8 L)			

LENGTH

⅛ in = 3 mm
¼ in = 6 mm
⅓ in = 1 cm
½ in = 1.5 cm
¾ in = 2 cm
1 in = 2.5 cm
1 ½ in = 4 cm
2 in = 5 cm
2 ½ in = 6 cm
4 in = 10 cm
8 in = 2 cm
10 in = 25 cm

TEMPERATURES

275˚F = 140˚C
300˚F = 150˚C
325˚F = 170˚C
350˚F = 180˚C
375˚F = 190˚C
400˚F = 200˚C
450˚F = 230˚C
475˚F = 240˚C
500˚F = 250˚C

OTHER CONVERSIONS

Ounces to milliliters: multiply ounces by 29.57
Quarts to liters; multiply quarts by 0.95
Milliliters to ounces: multiply milliliters by 0.034
Liters to quarts: multiply liters by 1.057
Ounces to grams: multiply ounces by 28.3
Grams to ounces: multiply grams by .0353
Pounds to grams: multiply pounds by 453.59
Pounds to kilograms: multiply pounds by 0.45
Ounces to milliliters: multiply ounces by 30
Cups to liters: multiply cups by 0.24

Artwork Credits

Page 1: bowls by Droll Designs.

Pages 7 and 8: plates by Julie Cline.

Page 10: plate by Cyclamen; napkin ring by Maugenest.

Page 12: plates by Matthew A. Yanchuk; background painting by Teri Sandison.

Page 13: cup by Reed Keller.

Page 18: footed bowl by Sylvia Wyler.

Page 23: plates by Julie Cline.

Page 25: mugs by Patricia Fay.

Page 28: plates by Margaret Grisz.

Page 30: Candlestick by Margaret Grisz and Curt Huddleston.

Page 32: plate by Susan Eslick.

Pages 33 and 34: platter by Eileen Goldenberg.

Page 36: plates by Barbara Eigen; glasses by Glass Improvement; napkin rings by Ooloo.

Page 37: cups and saucers by David Gurney.

Page 39: plates by Matthew A. Yanchuk.

Page 41: cups and saucers by Matthew A. Yanchuk.

Page 44: ceramics by T.S. Post; flatware by Sasaki.

Page 47: plate by Susan Eslick.

Page 52: plates by Cyclamen; chopsticks by Karyn Kozak.

Page 54: plates by Margaret Grisz.

Page 55: plate by Sylvia Wyler.

Page 58: platter by Eileen Goldenberg.

Page 59: cups by Eileen Goldenberg.

Pages 61 and 62: platter by Droll Designs.

Page 64: plate by Julie Cline.

Page 66: Plates by Eigen Arts; chopsticks by Karyn Kozak; napkin by Nancy Klion.

Page 67: bowls by Matthew A. Yanchuk.

Page 69: bowl by Margaret Grisz and Curt Huddleston.

Page 71: bowls by Matthew A. Yanchuk.

Page 74: platter by Droll Designs; spoon by Jonathan Simmons.

Page 76: cups by T.S. Post.

Page 78: bowl by Droll Designs.

Pages 81 and 82: bowls by Robin Spear.

Page 83: plate by Steinberg.

Page 86: bowls by Amy Danger.

Page 90: bowls by Robin Spear.

Page 93: plate by Gabrielle Schaffner.

Page 94: cups and saucer by Gabrielle Schaffner.

Page 96: bowls and plates by Margaret Grisz and Curt Huddleston.

Page 103: cups by Robin Spear.

Index